THE AYRSHIRE NESTLING

The Light Acknowledgers & Other Poems
(Happen*Stance* Press, 2019)
Notes for Lighting a Fire
(Happen*Stance* Press, 2012, hbk;
2013, 2nd edition, pbk)
Aves (Essence Press, 2007)
Madame Fi Fi's Farewell & Other Poems
(Luath Press, 2003)
*'Nothing But Heather!': Scottish Nature
in Poems, Photographs and Prose*
(Luath Press, 1999; 2nd edition, 2008)
The Shell House
(Scottish Cultural Press, 1995)

The Ayrshire Nestling

Gerry Cambridge

Tringa
Press

First published in 2024 by Tringa Press,
an imprint of Red Squirrel Press
36 Elphinstone Crescent
Biggar
South Lanarkshire
ML12 6GU
www.redsquirrelpress.com

Reprinted 2024

Layout, design and typesetting by Gerry Cambridge
e: gerry.cambridge@btinternet.com

ISBN: 978 1 913632 59 5

A CIP catalogue record for this book is available from
the British Library.

Red Squirrel Press and Tringa Press
are committed to a sustainable future.
This publication is printed in the UK by Imprint Digital
using Forest Stewardship Certified paper.

For Mireille Hanson

&

For Matt Bain:
in honour of our long friendship

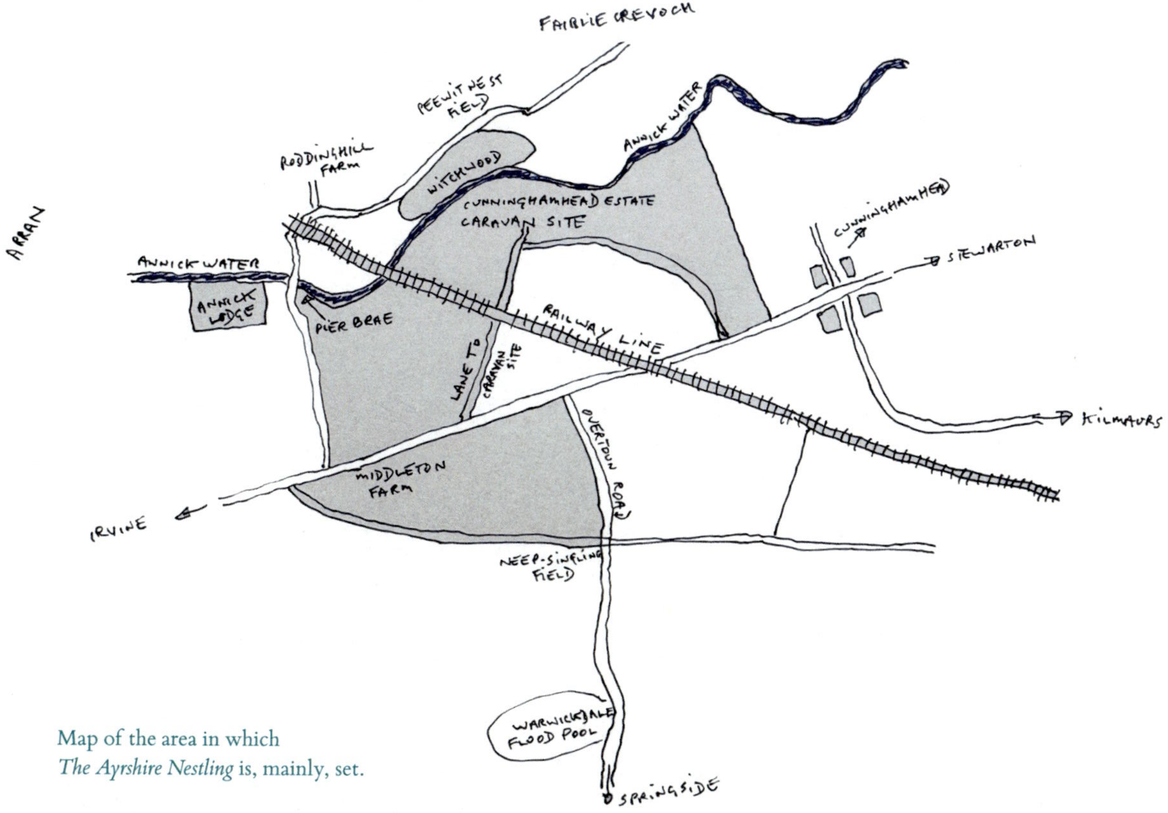

Map of the area in which
The Ayrshire Nestling is, mainly, set.

FAIRLIE CREVOCH

KILMAURS

TO STEWARTON

CUNNINGHAMHEAD

ANNICK WATER

CUNNINGHAMHEAD ESTATE
CARAVAN SITE

RAILWAY LINE

OVERTOUN ROAD

SPRINGSIDE

WARWICKDALE
FLOOD POOL

NEERSINKING
FIELD

MIDDLETON
FARM

LANE TO
CARAVAN SITE

PIER BRAE

WHITEHOUSE

REWIT NEST
FIELD

RODDINGHILL
FARM

ANNICK
LODGE

ANNICK WATER

RUINE

ARRAN

I T WAS NOVEMBER AND NOW they had arrived
and were trying to sleep. He was on the sofa in
the living room and the caravan had been left at an
odd angle so his head or his feet—whichever way
he tried it—were higher than each other. Squalls
rattled on the roof. There was whispering at first
but soon his sisters settled into steady breathing and,
further away, he could hear the snores of his father.

It was all new and strange again.

Somewhere in the dark, probably in the little
bedroom, held in a cardboard box among sawdust
smelling of pine, though he did not think of them
then, were the patterned eggshells of dozen of birds
he had brought with him, as light as air among the
fragrant wood, variously coloured and beautiful
and empty. Did they survive the journey? They
survived. They might have become birds but then
again they might not—hatched out only to be eat-
en, cowped down a crow's gullet or frozen on a first
night of enormous cold. But he had kept these safe,

at least, rapt when he raised the lid of the cardboard box onto their neat, lovingly arranged rows by a feeling he had no name for. It was beauty, and this was the only way he knew of having a part in it. He still saw it like that, though that would change.

Another shower rattled on the roof and soon, awkward and vulnerable and uncertain in this new world, he was asleep.

★

—You goin up, Oxy?

They stood at the bottom of the tree, all three faces upturned to where the big basket of twigs, right in the very treetop, swayed among the fresh lime of the new foliage.

—You goin up? He was the youngest. It was expected. The blond one with the rabbity teeth and the big quiet one with the red eruptions all over his face stood waiting.

—Okay. The first six or seven feet were without branches but he knew how to shimmy up, throwing his arms round the trunk as if he was hugging it and pushing upwards with his feet like swimming against the bark while relaxing his hold on the trunk. His feet slipped a couple of times, but he managed. Then he was among the first branches and it was mainly working out which to grab as he eased himself up among them, considering a route, while the ground slowly descended below him and the branches were rough against his palms and the twigs tickled and scraped his face as he moved upward with his heart thudding in his ears. The other two stood at the foot of the tree, talking quietly, occasionally gazing up together, two faces shrinking down there half-hidden by twigs. Up and up he went, the tree swaying in the breeze of the April evening, and shaken a little by his own weight, his climb gradually bringing him clear of the shorter trees around it so he could begin to see, beyond their leafy tops, fields and fields out to forever in the fresh harsh light. The clocks had gone forward just two weeks ago. Suddenly, as if a light had been switched on, it was spring.

He paused, panting, and the tree also settled as if it was responding to him, for he was in the upper branches now and the trunk had narrowed. He could see, below, the whinny bushes they said were full of linnet and yellowhammer nests, and the bit of pasture where they sometimes played football.

—Get up there! the blond one shouted. Yer no done yet! Blond one called him Oxy as a kind of joke. Blond one was buck-toothed and always going on about girls, recounting imagined pornographic scenarios in which the girls were, improbably, very nice to him. The other one, the big one, had something bad in him. His face was a mass of spots. Jed—Oxy—was frightened of him. He wouldn't be up this tree otherwise. It was too high for him and it only looked like a crow's nest. It wasn't worth the risk for a crow's nest. There were loads of them.

He looked up. The nest was ten feet above him now, precariously high almost in the top of the tree—a big basket of twigs among twigs and thin branches. He'd have to be careful. He was twelve but he was big for his age. His weight could snap things. Slowly, he began climbing again, and the top of the tree felt uneasily frail and weightless and airy. He was up in the full evening light now and once his right foot slipped and he hung, just for a second, before getting his foot on a slim branch. It was a long way down. They were both now watching him intently from the bottom: two faces, upturned, like saucers on a green table.

—Yer almost there, Oxy! shouted blond boy.

The tree top was now swaying considerably and alarmingly under his weight, the soft new leaves quivering on the twigs with each movement he made. His face was just below the big basket of twigs now. He found one last branch to stand on and then his face was level with the nest and then above it, looking down.

It was a crow's nest, with a big nesting cup about eight inches across made out of horse hair and sheep's wool. In its basket were three eggs, each a little smaller than a hen's. They were green as snot from your nose and freckled all over with dried-mud brown.

—Any eggs? shouted blond boy.

—No—empty! he shouted back down. If he had said there were eggs they'd have insisted he bring them one back down. The standard way was in your mouth. It was too easy to forget it was there, or you'd lose your concentration, and suddenly your teeth would crunch through the frailty of the shell and the viscous yolk and albumen slide down your throat before you had a chance to spit it out the way you spat the shell out in splinters and fragments, disgusted. He began the long descent. Five minutes later he had returned from the swaying upper dangerous airiness to the solidity of the ground under his feet, immense and reassuring when he leapt the last six feet to the ground, his feet thudding on the earth. He had proven he could climb a difficult tree.

★

When had it started? There had been a day in spring when a bunch of them had asked if he wanted to come along—a small gang of twelve-year olds. He remembered the big strawy nest of a blackbird in the hedge, the eggs like miniature crow's eggs (though he had not seen a crow's egg at that time)—one of the gang thrusting his hand and arm deep into the barbed thicket of the hawthorn with face grimacing, the bird having flown off in a burst of clucks, till he got his hand over the strawy rim. Eggs! he shouted. First! Second! Third! Fourth! they shouted, staking their claim. Sometimes one of them would shout *Bags I the freak!* It was a long time later he discovered that a laying bird sometimes ran out of pigment for its last egg, which was often paler and less marked than the others: the 'freak'. It was highly prized.

Sometimes they would try to blow the eggs using thorns immediately—a prick in the blunt end and the narrow end, and the egg held in the fingers and raised to your lips. Often it smashed, and the

PLATE 3.

BLACKBIRD & SONG THRUSH.

Stewart delt

Lizars sc.

jellies and blood of a little embryo lay glistening in the grass.

At first it was only blackbirds and song thrushes, the song thrushes' lined with dried mud, sometimes with little wood chippings in it, the four eggs blue as sky, tinily dotted with black and grey. Both species' were the same size, usually in haw bushes or hedges, easy to find, but the thrush had a speckled breast and both of them showed the strange intent look as they sat on the nest—their point of anchor to the earth. It made them vulnerable.

He didn't see it like that, though. They sat and as you put your hand towards them they hopped off the nest cup, among the thorns, and flew off with loud outraged cluckings. The eggs would be hot when you got your fingertips over the rim of the nest to touch them. You could tell by feel, more or less, how many, unless there were more than four when it just felt like a lot.

Once he had been introduced to the idea, he began going out by himself. This was the north of England. Industry abutted onto country. A big brickworks thundered beside the caravan site, the huge excavators day and night digging out the clay for the kilns; a mine bing overshadowed a village. But fields and woods and paths and bits of meadow in all their unpredictable variety were everywhere. He took to roaming. He bought two little books: the *Observer's Book of Birds*, that had colour plates of birds, with tantalising descriptions of the eggs and nests: colour, number; and the *Observer's Book of Birds' Eggs*, full of colour plates of the eggs themselves. He would be in his bedroom, looking through these. They were all outside, somewhere, if he could find them.

Blackbirds, thrushes; they were everywhere. Then one day in a little hedge up from the caravan, a smaller nest: moss, fine dried grass. Two eggs. A turquoisy, slightly greeny rich blue, no markings, and about half the size of a blackbird's or a thrush's. Something different. It was the small size that fascinated, the delicacy. It was late April and the light evenings: the world opening into summer. The rich unmarked blue of two little eggs in a nest held it all. For maybe half an hour he walked backwards and forwards up and down the hedge, peculiarly, for the pleasure of coming across the nest afresh with its two blue eggs. Finally he took one. The bird would lay others till there were four or perhaps five, then it would start to brood.

He carried the little blue egg in his hand, carefully, home and blew it out in the toilet. Even at that

PLATE 28

1 Song Thrush 2 Golden-crested Wren 3 Chimney Swallow 4 Common Wren 5 Jay 6 Kingfisher

age he was careful. It had to be done properly—reverently, even—in sequence. The egg was smaller than he was used to. He pricked a tiny hole in each end with a needle, raised it by the narrow end to his mouth, and blew, very gently. At first, nothing. Then a thread of clear albumen, followed, after some time, by the yolk's gold. You had to be careful: blow too strongly and the egg would burst in your fingers with the pressure of your breath. Not strongly enough, and its contents would stay firmly inside its blue oval.

And then he had it. It was heavier before but now it was light as air, no longer a thing of earth. His hands were filthy and his nails were bitten and he was a chaotic creature of appetite, but this was perfect and beautiful. The blue was beautiful. The size and the shape were beautiful, smooth as a pebble, with a lustre in the light. It was like a jewel, and he was rich.

It was a dunnock's egg—a hedge sparrow's. He lifted the lid of the cardboard box and added it to the blackbird's and song thrush's side by side in sawdust.

It was when he found his first chaffinch's nest, the next one in his growing list of discoveries, that for the first time he noticed especially the nest as well. It had little pieces of lichen woven into it and its perfect cup—how did the bird get it so perfectly round and neat?—was woven from what looked like the hair from horses' manes and pale fine grass. It was built among the shoots that had sprung from the side of a tree trunk, at hand level. He could walk straight up to it. And inside were four eggs in a little group—

nestled—together. The eggs were like nothing he'd seen before: a strange, muddy pinkish, with darker blotches, like dots of wet ink that had been rained on, just a little, so the ink had spread. That was at the edge of a wood beside where they played football in a bit of pasture, lumpy and tussocky, so the ball made unpredictable bounces, and with jerseys for goalposts, the pitch surrounded by whinny bushes. Then he discovered that these bushes were a virtual hotel or maternity wing for dozens of nesters—linnets, yellowhammers, grasshopper warblers. These three were of a whole other order of specialness. The linnets' were white with little darker brownish and blackish speckles and the smallest egg he'd seen so far. The yellowhammers' were bigger, with flourished lines and squiggles in black and almost violently dark purple. He could not be sure about the grasshopper warbler—the Observer's books said they were rare. But the egg was exactly like that in the book.

★

He learned a lot of things that year. He learned that with a pale, especially a white, egg, you could tell if it was fresh or 'dippy'—well incubated—by holding it up to the light between a thumb and forefinger. If it was fresh the light would pass through it and the yellow yolk gave the egg a pale gold glow. If it was well incubated with a chick inside it, the egg would be darker. Opaque, it would not transmit the light. He learned that if he fell in the whins when

PLATE 17.

MOUNTAIN FINCH

looking for nests, which he did often, or even to feel less pain going deep into a thicket of their spiky fibrous green armoury, if he relaxed his body and did not flinch it felt easier. Sometimes, months later, in his arms he found the little dark dots from which, when squeezed, a gorse thorn would rise vertically and slowly so he could grasp it and pluck it out. He learned that most of the small birds laid an egg a day for four, five or six days and then started to sit on them so they all hatched together. There were some nests and birds surrounded by an aura of indescribable glamour: buzzards; sparrowhawks; owls; none of which he'd ever seen. The first two he would not even have recognised if he had, because his focus wasn't on the birds, but on the eggs. Sometimes he'd hear of a bunch of boys going far away and discovering wild ducks' nests and moorhens' and coots' nests at a lake. Such tales, like that of someone finding a kestrel's nest, were the Shangri-La of his boyhood, promising the dream of the unexpected and the marvellous, experienced far away and brought back in a story.

No one told him that all this was wrong. It was 1971. Even old men sometimes went out looking for nests, though they would be less likely to take the eggs. An ex-miner took him and a friend out and showed him the best way to find skylarks' nests. It was to take a small dog with you that would 'flush' the bird as it sat on the eggs. This was in pastureland above a clay quarry where the massive yellow diggers, each like a dinosaur with huge thick tyres, howked out the clay in the metal jaws of their

PLATE 18.

COMMON BUZZARD

grab buckets. He remembered the nest, of delicate grasses, well-hidden in a tussock, and the pale eggs crowded with grey smudges and blotches. Miles up there, so high it was invisible, the bird would be singing, its notes particular and varying in the blue while its mate was hidden down here on the earth among tussocks on the four eggs. What was the fascination of it? The secret.

The same man also showed him a partridge's nest among dried tussocks in a bit of scrubby wasteground: the eggs olive-brown, pear-shaped, eight or nine of them at least, in a little hollow scrape lined with a few grasses. He did not want to ask if he could have one. When he went back later, by himself, he couldn't find the nest. It was as if it had vanished or was separated from him by another dimension.

Someone set fire to the whinny bushes. In the blackened, carbonned aftermath, fascinated and appalled, in the stink of burnt things, he walked through the incinerated remnants that charcoaled his mustard-coloured jersey. And there were the remains of the nests, too, some of them still with eggs that lay scattered and broken open on the ground below, some of them as if they'd been hardboiled, the tiny yolks solid like a hen's egg at breakfast, or the nestlings, featherless, scrawny, wide-beaked with gumsy brighter flanges, things of bony elbow, claw and protuberant belly, stiffened in death from the roar of flame that had crackled through the spiky green and yellow. He stepped out with hands blackened and smudged with carbon.

He remembered the first time he'd seen newly

hatched chicks—a blackbird's nest. The four ash-wisped, nude, transparent-skinned, gollum-ish gargoyles, the big skulls with their eye turrets of dark grey, something like a chameleon's, at the top of the skinny necks—how they all thrust up as one, swaying a little from side to side, mistaking his vibrations for an adult bird returning with food. The bright—were they yellow?—gumsy flanges on each side of the beak. The nestlings were like wizened old men, Tithonuses, but this was the start of life, not its end. They gave away their saurian ancestry. They were little growing machines. They had pot bellies, like men with skinny frames in late middle age. But what he found most amazing was that their skin was see-through. Through it you could make out, like small pieces of coloured plastic, their internal organs which, had he known these things, he could have identified. To these four fleshbags of appetite the adults would return, bead-eyed, beaks thick with worms slowly writhing and coiling and glistening in the light, to be thrust deep into the gaping maws.

The chicks grew, he learned, with astonishing speed. Twelve to fourteen days for a blackbird clutch to hatch; the same again for them to be ready to fly the nest. The ashy wisp-tufts would be superseded by feathers. On the wings the emerging quills looked like little paintbrushes at the tips. Soon you'd be met by four pairs of black-bead eyes, suspicious, over the nest rim. Then there'd be nothing there, but in the thorns around the nest, small sounds and the 'chink chink chink' of the adult, concerned for this new scattering.

★

He had taken to avoiding the small blond boy with
the rabbity teeth and the tall dark spotted one with
his face a morass of carbuncles, after hearing what
the latter had done, methodically, to a nest of baby
blackbirds. It would be many years later that he
would understand that the spotty youth—gangly
and repellent—was killing the weakness in himself, disgusted. Jed felt no such motive or desire. He
would take the eggs but if he was aware of cruelty
in this—which at that point he wasn't—there was
no impulse to inflict suffering. Rather, though he
could not have explained this then, it was that his
awe at the beauty of the objects outweighed what
was, potentially, growing inside them. For at that
point a goldfinch singing on a treetop was simply
an abstraction. The gorgeousness of the nest, the
chalice for the four, or six, pale eggs specked with
brown and black in that particular way that said
only *goldfinch, goldfinch, goldfinch*, interwoven in the
twigs of a high thornbush and swaying in the May
breezes, the little bird sitting snug on it like a lid,
and the grunting, panting, face-scratched boy, were
real. Many years after, when such things were genu-
inely taboo and had mainly passed, as far as he knew,
into history, he would wonder why, when news
items announced this or that egg collector had been
found with 5,000 rare birds' eggs—police raids—secret cabinets—it was almost always men found to
be the guilty party, slapped down with big fines or
even prison sentences. Was it 'egg envy'? For him,

PLATE 16.

Stewart delt.   Lizars sc.

GOLDFINCH.

despite the results which in later life he would consider guiltily, it was a veneration of beauty, a need to possess it. And where did this need come from?

He was avoiding small blond one and big spotted one, though they had told him that the girl he sometimes encountered walking alone along the paths, still in her school blazer and grey skirt, was being courted and secretly meeting someone who the blond boy called 'The Rock' because when he took his shirt off his torso looked solid as granite. He was older, had left school, and even had a job—he worked in a garage, and was thus surrounded with an air of mystique and allure. Once, Jed encountered the girl. That was on the path above the caravan site where there was a mistle thrush's nest he daren't climb to, despite their clutches being buff-coloured with salmony and brown markings a world apart from the song thrush's blue eggs: mistle thrushes were known for attacking you. She stopped and spoke to him, a very little, though he did not remember what she said, only the manner of its saying, which was vaguely teasing, as if she knew some great secret that he would be the better for knowing too, except he didn't. Sometimes she would sit in front of him on the school bus. She had pale gold hair that fell halfway down over her shoulders and a fine aquiline nose. There were blonde squiqqles of hair cast by her brushing stuck to the dark blue of her blazer all down her back like hieroglyphs. Her blouse would be white. Her school tie was striped. In ways he did not understand then she was connected with the smashed shells and blood and jellies in the fingers of the boys trying to blow out blackbirds' eggs, and with him.

★

The huge brickworks beside the caravan site. In his imagination this would be recalled as like something out of Gotham city, an affair of pipes and metal staircases and bulb-light, deafening with clankings and wheezings. With another boy he went in there once looking for sparrows' nests, only to be chased by shouts and a man quickly descending a metal staircase, his hand on the rail. At the edge of this brickworks were a whole series of kilns—not a word he would have used then—which would have their entrances sealed up periodically with bricks, to bake the bricks inside. Then they would be taken down and the new bricks within, after some days to let them cool, removed. Once, he and another boy went into the empty kiln—a long chamber with an arched top, a dry chamber of red dust, lit by bulb-light, still with some bricks stacked at the end. A Mars on earth. They climbed the bricks on the small ladder leaning against them and discovered that the further back in the kiln and closer to the ceiling you got the rarer and hotter the atmosphere and the harder it was to breathe. They took turns seeing who could stay up there longest. The utter dryness and stillness, the red dust, the bulb-light, his head just under the roof. The air was so parched, so airless, that you could only inhale shallowly, feeling the hot airlessness drying up the inside of your lungs and their moisture you hadn't been aware of before, until it met this other thing, its opposite. There was the sense of a dare in being so far into the radiant kiln against its furthest wall. You were tempting the opposite of life. They ran out again, into the swabbing smirriness of a May evening, met by the wave of great kind coolness, taking big gulps of it into their boyhood lungs.

★

His egg collection grew; the mother bird that was his obsessiveness kept adding eggs in various colours and patterns to the nest: an old cardboard box now filled with sawdust that had held a winter coat. A collection of jewels in a plush casket would have been less precious to him than this grouping of birds' eggs, arranged in their neat rows, with the tiny imperceptible pinpricks at each end—the tinier the better—where the egg had been blown. Sometimes the hole in one end had to be larger and this meant the egg was less precious to him, to be replaced in time by a better one if he could. There was less patterned shell then and more reminder of what it had contained. How light they were! You could put ten of them—some were small enough for you to imagine this—on your palm and believe, if you tossed them into the air, they would simply float off, like thistle seeds carried on the summer breezes. When, later, he encountered dragonfly exuvia—the cast nymphal skins of the newly hatched insects—clinging to reeds at pond margins on summer mornings he would be reminded of this light fragility, how easily all that intricacy was crushable into fragments by the strength of fingers. They were mainly passerine eggs—yellowhammer, reed bunting, swallow, sand martin, blue tit, great tit, willow tit—with some bigger ones: moorhen, pheasant, crow. They were more precious than gemstones because they were the book of his days told in the splendid various colours and patterns, the visual encyclopaedia of that part of his life. They were a record of death though he did not wish this to be so. Everything was a record of death, like the writhing, glistening pink meat of the worms thrust deep into the gullets of blackbird chicks so that later the male could flute from a bough on an April evening with his gold beak and gold eye-ring and rich black. Death would eat them all, but for now he had this rich shining dazzle between two darknesses, except the dazzle was all there was.

★

It was May. All across that landscape, where the natural and the industrial bled into each other, new life was starting. In hundreds of nests dotted and hidden in hedges and scrub and tussocks and tree boles and twig tops and in brambly thickets, the eggs were growing darker and heavier with life, the tiny yolks were ramifying through with the small red lightnings of capillaries, the embryo reptiles, cell by cell, hour by hour, were coalescing and forming and gathering in their thousands as the sun rose, inexorably, day after day, higher, indifferently strengthening over whatever heartbreak and brutality, and hundreds of sweaty, carnivorous wee boys, snottery and avaricious and deadly, roamed the countryside looking for nests. Another old trick, to find out if an egg was 'dippy', with an embryo inside, was to drop it into a cup or glass of water. If it sank, it was fresh. If it floated, it had been well incubated. It seemed counter-intuitive that an egg without a bird in it would sink, and one containing one would float, till he read that as the chick inside develops it pulls away from the egg's inner membrane at one end and makes an air pocket so the bird can breathe in the egg in the first minutes of its chipping its way out of the shell. For death is heavy, while life is light; yet it does not let the rays pass through. The spring was clear and harsh and he was aware at some subliminal level of the starkness of it, but it was only later that he would come to realise viscerally the necessary unavoidable vulnerability if anything was to exist at all. Even as an adult, many years later, certain atmospheres of a spring evening, when the world was loosening and creaking in its joints after the long seized-upness of winter, particular qualities of the light, or a blackbird melancholily fluting from a tall tree, would bring it back to him: it was a purely pragmatic world, one without emotion or gentleness. It was manifested for him—he thought, as an adult—by eggs in a nest and a bird sitting on them in its implicating biological urge, then the complete helplessness of the nestlings, nude and primitive under the whole sky, vulnerable to the whims of arbitrary power. It was staking its claim, that sitting bird, like all of them, against the future and what might happen. And the sun rose and activated everything, day on day, the magician of rays, the photon king.

★

Then they had moved and there was no more of all that, or of the other youngsters, mad and lively as a bunch of sanderlings before a crashing wave or as starlings on a lawn. It was Scotland; November. He did not even know where he was in the country called 'Scotland', except his granddad, his father's dad, had lived there and they had gone to see him once or twice when he was a little boy. A grim figure in a big chair. The stench of an old man's concentrated rich amber when he rose to pee in the middle of the night in a bedroom, long in shadow and forgotten now, which they must have shared. A cream semmit. An old Lanarkshire miner's white chest hairs sprouting and curling up over its top edge. It would all be forgotten, all the red griefs and agonies honeyed and dried and turned to story by centuries. Names eroded from gravestones staggered by decades. Mountains become grains of sand.

The first time they had come to Scotland they had brought their wee dog, Patch, with them. In the early-hour darkness they crossed the border from England. Patch vomited in his lap in the back seat. 'That's us, we're in Scotland now', his father had announced. Scotland was wee dogs vomiting in wee boys' laps.

Now they had come back for good. He knew nothing. Bar the country they were in, he could not have told you on a map where he was. It was a small caravan site set in Ayrshire countryside. On the long lane up to it, the afternoon they arrived, with a few small ramps on the tarmac at the entrance, someone had hand-scrawled a 'T' in front of the last word on the BEWARE OF RAMPS sign as you entered the site itself.

Language. They were four miles outside the town of Irvine—he called it 'Ir-*vine*', rhyming with 'mine' at first, until corrected. No, it was 'Ir-vin', rhyming with 'sin', but the stress on the first syllable. The first of many corrections. 'Pop', lemonade, was called 'ginger'. A bag of chips was a poke of chips. You did not 'live' in a particular town; you 'stayed' in it. 'Where d'you stey?'—where d'you live? Far in his future, about a landscape he would have come then to know like his own body, he would experience a famous writer correcting his pronunciation of where he was from. 'Cunninghamhead' he'd said. 'Cunninghamheid,' the famous writer said. A small linguistic rap on the knuckles. *Who owns a landscape?* Norman MacCaig asked. The one who claims it by changing a vowel, or the one who can tell you where the tawny owl has nested in it for the last three years? The rich, contrary ironies of being here. Who had the prior claim? The famous writer correcting the young man? Who had the truer? The young man who had worked singling neeps for old Davy Smith of Middleton? Reflecting on this many years later the changed vowel was a skelf needling him but he also felt, within him, rage. His claim was love's. The other's claim was, he might have thought, a cheap political point. But behind it, for all that, was centuries of history, a history which was not his and which he could not lay a claim to, unlike those fields' and woods' and hedgebacks' natural history which was free, at some level, of the blood and agony of human centuries. The one steeped in human pain, the other a thing, as he saw it, of light and Latin and unimplication. It was all there in a changed vowel. In old age, far in his future, he would sometimes still think about it, surprised by the flood of emotion it released in him.

★

Now he was standing outside the rector's office— 'Fat Chick' as he discovered he was called—to be seen. The secretary had taken his details in the office opposite. He had been in third year in school in the north of England. So they put him into third year here, when, owing to the different systems, he should have been in second year.

—What are your subjects? the secretary asked him.

He did not know what his subjects were. He hadn't chosen any yet. He hadn't even thought about it. English and Arithmetic were compulsory. The others, barring timetable clashes, you could choose. So on the spot, he chose Chemistry, Biology, Geography, French, Woodwork.

A girl waiting outside Fat Chick's office had spoken to him friendlily. —What are you here for? she asked.

—I'm new, he said.

—I'm here for not doing what they want, she said, answering the question he had been too shy to ask.

It was November. England had had miniskirts and the girls burgeoning like late summer apples. In Scotland the girls all wore midiskirts, well down below the knee. There were no thrilling glimpses for him of pale blue or white or pink. Everything was much more serious—maybe because he was suddenly among a group a year older, but not just that. It was an aspect of the country too.

The Parish Priest visited one day, curious and slightly concerned when he learned he had not gone to St Michael's in Kilwinning but to Irvine Royal Academy, which was closer.

—Have you experienced any trouble?

He lied and said he had not.

(He was wary as a heron of the black garb and the white collar. He had an instinctive fear of the oppression of the institution. Even when he was younger he remembered in the confessional the rehearsed litany of respectable sins in the mothball-smelling cubicle with the priest's deep voice behind the grille. *Bless me, Father, for I have sinned. It's been ten weeks since my last confession.* Behind it, he felt instinctively, even if he did not know it intellectually, was the whole weight and power and oppression of the hierarchy of the Catholic Church, filled with obeisant conformity structured and hardened out of the original insights of a first genius. The little box with the kneeling child and the priest sitting sideways-on, dimly visible in profile behind the grille, was the needle point of all that magnificence, gathered wealth, and worldly power. He was tiny there as a comma in a book or an atom of carbon in a dinosaur but he could outwit it by not giving them his inner life. The recitation of the safe, respectable sins. Not how he had felt at that glimpse, white as a linnet's egg, involving Lynne Witherspoon. Nothing of blood and albumen. Perhaps, he would later think, he was an instinctive Protestant.)

★

—Have you experienced any trouble? the priest had said.

He said he had not. It was where the doubleness of his life began. Down the long lane from the caravan site in the mornings for the school bus at 8.20am, the single decker green bus from Stewarton to Ayr. There wasn't another, if you missed it, for an hour, which was *real trouble*. You could see it, though, from the vantage of the lane, quarter of a mile away to the left approaching ominously at the crest of the road at Cunninghamhead crossroads— time enough to sprint from there to the lane end before it appeared through the last stand of trees on the left down there, and travelling fast. He would be shouting to his two sisters and foster-brother— Bus! The bus! They would have gone on ahead because they were smaller and slower, sometimes with his mother. There were mornings of clattering gales and squalls, their coats flapping, gloves and his sisters' shrieks being blown away, when the gusts strewed the wet tarmac of the lane with bits of twigs, and the turning leaves, buttery and russet on the soaked black, were startled to brilliance by the panning light.

That was where the doubleness began. His sisters and brother would leave for the bus five minutes before him. It was the first distancing. Then they would be standing together, but not together, when the bus suddenly appeared over the rise on the last straight before it slowed at the lane end and its blue sign—Cunninghamhead Estate Caravan Park. The terrifying bus in the terrifying world, and the moments when you didn't know if it would stop, even, till there was a sense of it slowing and it stopped and you all got in, breathless if you'd been running to catch it, in a flurry of touslement and disarray, out of the clattering autumn weather. He would sit right up at the back. His oldest sister and her two charges sat near the front. Every morning, many of the same passengers. The youth from Perceton Row, muscly and mannish already in fifth year, solid and silent.

Jed would get off at Irvine Cross, two stops before the others. A nod, a muttered goodbye as he passed them and if he was safe to, if no one he knew or might know, who might know someone else, could see this more than cursory acknowledgement and infer a connection. When he stepped out onto the pavement, he was alone again, unattached and unimplicated, and could breathe.

Duality, the shaming denial. He became aware

that first winter of a big secret he carried that, quite inexplicably to him, he represented. He was it; his body and his existence made it so.

Irvine Royal, for reasons he did not think about, was divided into two, connected by a walk across an elevated metal bridge, from which you could see Bogside mudflats. Beside the older part was the Catholic primary school where his sisters and foster brother went. The Biology classroom for Irvine Royal was in the playground of this primary school. He could not remember exactly how his awareness that there was something unacceptable in him had started, though one day he had been walking with a friend of his behind a wee girl on her way to the primary school. The friend was the son of a prominent figure in the town. Jed admired his physique, a natural athleticism that broadened his blazered shoulders. Suddenly his friend had begun muttering, loud enough to be heard by the wee girl, 'Pape, pape, pape, pape!' 'Pape, pape-pape-pape!'—increasing in tempo. Jed had said nothing, and the wee girl had run on, voiceless, ahead.

He was the vessel and locality of this big secret. He would try and avoid going to the Biology classroom until the very last minute in case, as he stood outside waiting, one or other of his sisters at their playtime would come up to him—like normal children. There would be questions asked. There would be connections made. He could be exposed at any point. At school's end, his sisters and brother got on at the same stop they'd disembarked at in the morning. He would get on two stops later, at Irvine Cross.

An inbuilt separation. A nod or a brief greeting if it was possible and he would sit at the back of the bus. Every stop outward back to Cunninghamhead was a movement toward civilisation, or at least civility. At the bottom of the lane he would hoist his little brother up onto his shoulders and, grasping the two small hands in his big ones, jog up the slope, released into an allowed familiarity again. Laughter. Breathless squeals of secure faux-terror. There was the life off the bus, of easy familiarity, and the life of the school and the town, the life of denial.

The secret shadowed his life. He lay in bed at night wrestling with it. It was human history and he knew nothing about it. It was simply how things were. He did not, at that point, connect present with past. Instead he escaped into the fields and the woods. Natural history. This was the only green and blue he loved. It was freedom. It was a clear space. It was only itself, it did not come like an old man dragging the blood-soaked past with it. It was light as a sunbeam like that which would later slant-shine into the caravan kitchen on April mornings, Neil Sedaka singing out on Radio 1 about a brighter day.

He learnt a lot of things at Irvine Royal that first winter. Movements of unpredictable sudden violence passed through the adolescent boys in third year like a current along a cable. Often he escaped this because of his size but not always. One movement took the form of instant, unannounced, full-strength karate chops to the Adam's apple. Another was a jab with knuckles or pointed fingers to the solar plexus. Another, a completely unexpected kick

to the scrotum—a 'tok in the balls'. Some of the
boys would whinny like a bleating display-flighting
snipe at the merest suggestion of homosexuality on
the part of another. He remembered a shopkeeper's
son, rich on steak, kidneys, liver, red-faced and pus-
tular with custard yellow, delivering unexpectedly
one such 'tok' to another boy, who dropped like a
stone and lay curled in agony on the schoolground
tarmac while the perpetrator paraded round, pea-
cockish in his heavy brown brogues and blazer,
whinnying in absurd caricature. There was another
teenager there who had the worst case of teenage
acne he had ever seen. Every day must have been an
agony of bearing the front of his face out into the
noticing world. For some reason, this boy seemed to
take against Jed. One day in the gym the boy casu-
ally, and without looking, as they stood facing out
together side by side, swung his arm out sideways
and struck him full on the side of his face with the
back of his hand, a fixed rictus of a white-toothed
smile set in the teenager's devastated complexion
as Jed saw when he looked at him. Jed did not respond. He did not even say anything. He simply
accepted it. His lack of response would have been
more cowardly than it was had he felt offended. In
fact, he was simply puzzled. And one part of him
felt sorry for the boy and superior to him. His own
face was at that point relatively unmarked, not like
the angry mass on the other's face. He could afford
not to respond. There was a further boy, small and
tykish, who also took against him when Jed had to
make a team up in the gym, and writing everyone's
name down on a sheet had spelt the boy's surname

wrongly. Ridicule. Thereafter this boy would bait
him sometimes—throw pellets of paper at him from
behind if they were walking down a corridor, or apple cores would fly past his head outside. He never
responded, though he might have had he been hit.
One day he was walking down the corridor to the
Geography class, carrying the stuffed satchel under
his right arm. His antagonist was in the corridor and
tried to stop him. 'Hey! Gees one o yer jotters! Ah
forgot mine!'

Jed was late and in a hurry and he did not slow.
The other thrust his leg across his path to try and
stop him. Jed simply continued at his hurried pace,
and the boy's thrust out leg had as little effect on his
momentum as a winter umbellifer stalk. He was left
sprawling on his back in the corridor. Jed turned to
the left into the class and sat at his usual desk near
the front, full of foreboding during the lesson for
later consequences. Strangely, his adversary never
bothered him again.

One day word spread through the school that a
body had been seen in the river Irvine. Crowds of
animated teenagers at lunchtime gathered in Irvine
Shopping Mall over the river, for a glimpse. It was
still there, just below the surface, swaying a little,
bent around a branch at the waist, hair stream-
ing out, and weed, in the river's current, the skin
white and bloodless as the moon. He went with a
group, and also looked a little, baffled and without
the thrilled excitement that had many of the others
chattering like winter starlings before a roost. That
was Irvine Royal, the school where he first experienced the love of the world.

★

Winter to Spring: the silent speeding of the planet on its ellipse around the sun; the light dangerously lengthening. He had been able to go to 6pm Mass confident of undetection in the darkness. There was only the brief exposure to electric light crossing the car park in front of the chapel, the glary illumination of its entrance, both entering and leaving, when he might be seen. He liked owls, the thought of owls— he had not yet seen a real, live one: haunters of the shadows. Three of his closest friends, including Robert, a cheery boy with tously curls the colour of a carrot, lived in West Road, the chapel's road.

Inside, the little bony pious priest, white-haired, rigid with abstinence and bodily control. The wooden pews, the kneeling, the standing, the obeisance, the awkward embarrassment of 'Let us offer each other the sign of peace...'—turning to shake the hands (though you could get away with just one handshake) of complete strangers. The head-down awkwardness as the purple plush faux-velvet of the collection bag passed by, with no clink of tossed coins from you hitting the others in the bottom. It was better, though, than the open collection plate, where your miserliness or otherwise, and thus your heathenness or otherwise, could be exposed and censoriously noted.

Then it was the concealing darkness of the back-seat of the car again and the speeding out beyond the town lights into the silent countryside and the caravan site to an illusory safety.

There was only one other boy on the caravan site. He had seen him, that first morning, on the blustering walk down the lane for the bus, accompanied by his mother. He was smaller than Jed and sported red soles on his shoes with the prints of particular animals embossed in the soles' plastics. He had a petulant and entitled air. But there was no one else to befriend. An only child with a doting and indulgent mother; his cheerful father, confident and renowned, he would later discover, for his strength. Thirty-five years later all three would be dead.

Somehow Jed had shown him his egg collection and the other boy, too, became interested in birds' eggs. Briefly there was a prickling of competition between them. He disliked competition because it made him do things he would not otherwise, but he was stirred by it. The other boy got a swan's egg: the size of it, the pale unmarked green, the thickness of the shell, when he held it; but he wouldn't tell him from where.

The types of nests Jed found changed in this different landscape. A jackdaw's in a tree hole, eggs a beautiful light bluey-green, differently marked from the usual crow's egg. A wren's nest, built in the hanging pale grasses that depended like a thick fringe below the entrance to a culvert that ran below the railway embankment. Its nest was different: the entrance hole on the side, about two thirds of the way up; a thing of moss and grasses, softly lined, the bird whirring like a little moth from the entrance hole and into a nearby thicket when he shook the nest. His fingers inserted, their tips encountering

PLATE 23.

WREN.

the hot clutch, and gently retrieving with care, lest it break, a single egg: white, tiny, constellated with rust or blood. On a ledge below the aqueduct of the railway line, a blackbird's nest. Some bird had made a fresh lining in its stout strawiness. Then there was an egg: small, brownish: *The Observer's Book of Birds' Eggs* said: Grey Wagtail. 'Their nesting site is usually near a stream, the nest being built in a hollow in a bank, a wall, or among rocks; it consists of grass, leaves, moss and roots, lined with hair and sometimes a few feathers.'

He would leaf through the little pages of this pocketsized volume. How come a willow tit's egg was so different from a coal tit's egg? How come a chaffinch's was so different from a greenfinch's? How come so many of them were so small, and delicate, and different from each other? How come they existed in the world at all? They were all arranged in colour plates in pairs across the tops of the pages of this 50-pence book, like precious stones in a shop catalogue. Except they might all be out there somewhere—he thought of all the woods and fields around him—and they cost nothing. This came to him less as a sense of greed realised than as fascination. He would devour the factual poetry in the little accounts: 'There are three clutches in a year, with four or five eggs in each clutch. The ground colour is a beautifully clear pale greenish-blue—almost turquoise—and the markings consist of specks, spots and blotches of a very deep olive-green, black or reddish brown.' This was the song thrush's. What right did he have to have 'almost turquoise' in his

GREY WAGTAIL.

STEWART del.

PLATE 10.

life? What had he done to deserve it? He would make his way through the pages, delighted and re-assured that he had some of these eggs already and excited by the exoticism and rarity and glamour of many that, he knew, he probably never would see— the far high ranges of unexpectedness and astonish-ment: Razorbill! Arctic Tern! Stone Curlew! Great Crested Grebe! Garganey! Gadwall! Merlin! He was only a boy in an Ayrshire caravan but somehow he could be a part of this and be lost in it.

He developed a mental map of the whole area around where he lived, the complexities of the lit-tle piece of landscape, every hawthorn bush, every rooty slope, every field edge that he had come to and been thrown together with at that particular point in time: the endless intricacy of it all! The caravan site was in what was left of a walled garden. He would dip out through the exit in the stone masonry, down the track through hazel saplings that led down to-wards the river, the Annick Water, that you could hear, gradually intensifying as you descended: live water running over stones and boulders. He did not know it then but almost fifty years later he could hold this landscape up in his mind like a great jewel, turning it this way and that, watching the light catch it and all its facts and details, and still be astonished. The Witchwood over the Annick Water, the fields beyond Fairliecrevoch, the walk along the river val-ley to the Pier Brae and the forbidden woods of the Annick Lodge estate, the Moss further over beyond the fields of Fairliecrevoch near Girgenti Farm with its clocktower, the damp marshy hollow full of

PLATE 17

THE RASOR BILL

PLATE 24

COMMON THICK-KNEE

snipe and duck that the farmer Malcolm Wilson, the big tall blond man, had drained for ploughing the sumptuous brown-black soil.

A railway line ran past the caravan site, at one point passing under the long drive from the main road up the hill to the site entrance. He would walk this line, drawn by the brambly and thickety embankment sides full of whitethroats and sedge warblers and yellowhammers in the spring. Sometimes he would pace it for miles, usually in only one direction which drew him because, mile by mile, it kept his interest, walking along the gleam of rails across the big dark wood of the splintery sleepers that were set just that little too close together for his natural long strides for comfort, so he would have to shorten the length of his steps and adopt a faster, less roomy gait than his instincts dictated. Sometimes for respite from this he would walk on the big grey whinstone pebbles on either side of the track, or in the middle (between the two sets of tracks), until the sharpness and irregularity of the stones sent him back to his short-stepping quick gait down the rails. It was forbidden to be on the rails of course, he would have known if he'd thought about it, as taking birds' eggs was forbidden too, but no one talked about it. The tracks narrowed into the distance, converging to a point that seemed very far off and you had to be constantly on the lookout for a train approaching from either direction. Was that one? You'd narrow your eyes ahead like a castaway conjuring a horizon ship except here there was something sinister in the approach of the tons of metal and wheels speeding along the gleaming tracks. It would be here soon. The trains that came from behind you were harder to notice. You might hear them through the rails, like some intimation of an event full of danger. They made a sound, an undertone of metal being compressed far off under the huge weight of great wheels, yet present with you.

It would be here soon and you'd see it enlarging imperceptibly at first as it was coming at you head-on, but then its arrival would be unignorable and you'd duck into the side of the track as hidden as possible as the great thundering mass swept by, lifting your hair in the gust of its passing, and clattering off with diminishing sound into the distance so you could go back to the silent line, secure that there might be no more trains for an hour or two. For many years later he would have dreams about the distant approach of a train, an intimation of something huge and potentially dreadful arriving.

★

The planet roared through space; its great curve, with him on it, and the caravan site, and all the nests and birds' eggs, the woods, rivers and fields, and his sisters and brother, were swung slowly out through the small hours on the morning he decided he was getting up to go and look for peewits'—lapwings'— nests. There was the egg in his book—unlike anything else he'd ever seen: shaped like a pear, brownish, darker blotched and dotted. They made their nests on the ground, the little book said, among a few straws in a scrape in the soil.

He had set an alarm early—4am—a time he'd probably never been awake before—pulled on his clothes quickly, and without tea or breakfast let himself out quietly, moving gingerly so as not to disturb his sleeping sisters. He did not want a human voice breaking into the silence of what he was doing. And there was no one he could tell in any case. He knew he would not be missed. He would be back before anyone else was even awake.

He unlocked the door of the caravan, and slipped out, onto the raised step at the door which formed a little makeshift balcony anyone visiting could stand on while they waited for a response to their knock of enquiry. After the warmth of the bedclothes and the oblivion of sleep, the chill damp shocked him into greater alertness. He had pulled on, quickly, a thick jersey. Everything was grey, pewter; mist was hanging in the valleys in the strengthening light. He descended the step and took the back way, ducking out through the exit doorway in the old wall. The dawn chorus was just starting up. In that huge country silence, without even a car at the lane end passing to disturb it, the birds were tuning up, like some strange avian orchestra lit by what was going to happen. As it gathered in intensity, the songs of chaffinches, blackbirds, song thrushes, robins, hedge sparrows, woodpigeons, with their notes particular and distinguishable in the foreground, all merged into the distance over at Annick Lodge westward— a huge sea of songbird sound diminishing off among the woods and boughs and twigs in the west.

WOOD PIGEON

He took the mudded track down to the Annick
Water valley, turned right at the bottom opposite
the ruin of the white house, and scrambled down
the bank to the river edge, among the watery musics
at the point where the river ran a little shallower
over rocks and boulders. Scraps of mist sat across the
valley on the other side. The water ran a little louder
over the rills at that point. In the nondescript dawn
he gauged his route, boulder to boulder, and began
to leap across, stopping once in the middle, teetering
on a mossy stone, then leaping again. You had to
be careful—one wrong step and one of your legs
would slip off a boulder and be in the water, up to
the knee in it: the shock of cold and the sopping wet
as you half-leapt, half-staggered, cursing, across to
the opposite bank. If you got wet it was discomfort
for at least an hour. So he planned his route before
setting off from the bank—that boulder, then this

(was it wet and slippery, though?), then that. And so on, using all your reserves of nimbleness and balance, till you were at the other side.

He passed quickly across without mishap, and was up the other side, across the pasture where the cows were grazing—they only lifted their heads and looked at him dully as he passed—through the dewed tussocks and up the wooded slope that, at its top, led to the other lane that, if you turned right, took you to Fairliecrevoch; if left, to Roddinghill. But he was going to neither. He slipped across the lane, though the hedge bordering it, and was into the field of newly-seeded barley, the green shoots just starting to spear through the soil. The torn, ragged cries of peewits greeted him, some, further off in the misty light and lost in it, display-flighting males: up close, the peewit's voice was peculiar: throaty and guttural, half-soprano, half-smoker's wheeze, trying to be melody, with a note of pain in the alarm call: it *sounded* like alarm.

They were nesting here somewhere, all across the curve of this barley field. He began quartering it in the strengthening light with his head down, eyes focused on the ground a few yards in front of him. The planet was turning, lifting the sun in imperceptible stages, and the earth slowly woke like a sleeping face gradually coming to consciousness.

It did not take him long to find the first nest—the four eggs all with their pointed ends facing into the centre, like the points of triangles, the most efficient use of space so the bird could warm them all together, tranferring its body heat to the cold inert yolks

GREEN LAPWING OR PEEWIT.

PLATE 25.

and albumen inside, stirring them into coalescing life. It was a form of magic but he did not think like that in the mist of the morning, when peewits appeared in and out of the grey overhead, with their torn-off, melancholy, harrowed cries or stood at some distance away on a rise, the long recurved crest visible, the bird calling out querulously with vigilant concern.

He bent to the scrape and touched the warmth of the eggs, so alive in the cold grey dawn. You were still allowed to take peewits' eggs to eat before April 15th, but despite that and maybe because a clutch with only three eggs in it and not four in a peewit's nest would look all wrong, he didn't take an egg. Instead he stood, and in his mind made a marker point in two directions to find the nest again if he needed to: that point in that fence; that raised twig in the hawthorn hedge. Then he went on, still looking.

That morning he found four peewits' nests across the field. The eggs were beautiful, like living pebbles. By the time he left, taking the longer way back, along the lane towards Roddinghill then left along the railway line, then left over the stone dyke and up across the two fields to the caravan site, the sun like an orange showing weakly through the dawn haar. He had been awake for two hours.

He let himself quietly into the kitchen of the sleeping caravan. He stripped off quickly and eased under the covers. It was 6am and it felt like noon. Before long, with a mind full of dawnlight and peewits' nests, eggs, and torn-off cries, he was asleep. No one had known he had been anywhere and come back. It was his secret and he held it to himself as he drifted off, exhausted at fourteen while the great planet stirred with its ancient energies. Even at that age, he knew the earth was a stronger thing than him.

★

—Wake up. You've got Mass today.

It was the first thing his father said that morning. He always made it sound like a punishment, something to be endured. As, for him, it was. It was Good Friday—why was it called 'good' when it was all about a man being crucified?—and the landscape around the caravan site was starting to show its singular beauty. But there was more than that to it. There was a harsh and savage exhilaration in the life force that had all these birds' eggs being laid, all these wildflowers thrusting up out of the earth, all these buds swelling and readying to burst into leaf. There was a pain in all that birth that he must have been vaguely aware of but that, at fourteen, he did not see fully as he was a part of those energies creaking themselves and flexing and loosening the vice-locks of the long winter, like some absurd caricature of David Banner, the Hulk, about to go through one of his transformations. It was birth happening, and that was pain. The light in its new brilliance was a beautiful blade.

And today was Good Friday with its long 3pm service. He woke to blue, clear skies, and the sun rising into it, the peaks of Arran in the Firth of Clyde, visible westward beyond the woods of Annick Lodge, vaguely Himalayan and without a cloud troubling their tops. It was going to be a stunning day, and he hated it. The external beauty of the world, for all its glary brilliance, put into deeply ironic contrast the slum of his mind with its knowledge he had to go to chapel—for he was still not able to openly rebel.

'As long as you're in this caravan you'll obey my rules,' his father had told him. He was stuck. He had no money, power or possibility. All he could do was be acted upon by this man who seemed to hate him and resent the position he held in the eyes of his mother—a firstborn son, a Catholic mother. His answer was to escape, as often as possible and for as long as possible, across the fields. The woods and fields and thickets out there were his saviour. They were the large-bedroom refuge he did not have.

But today there was no escape. They would leave at 2.30pm, when the heat and the light and the beauty were at their peak. He had to put on a shirt and tie, noosing it around his neck: clean stiff clothes; polished shoes. This was the worst day of the year. There were peewits nesting out in the fields. On the Annick Water, unspated and running dark and low in the dry weather, a moorhen had made a nest on a boulder in the middle of the river out of strawy bits of thick grass that the floods left deposited on the banks on either side. He already had a moorhen's egg, buff with its little black and lilac and brown smudges, and he liked just to watch the bird. He could have been wandering out under the sky in the April sunlight, free, in his loose clothes and his boots.

COMMON GALLINULE

PLATE 32

Instead he was in the heat of the back of the car with his girning siblings, being driven to Irvine to risk discovery when he stepped out in the chapel carpark in West Road, and then again afterwards when they all emerged from the chapel at the service's end. The town was busy. All his schoolfriends could be around, somewhere. He would not know if he'd been seen unless there was a question when he was back at school. *Hey, Jed, what were you doin goin into St Mary's? You a Pape?*

His father seemed to take the oppressed's grim satisfaction in the oppression of someone else. Inside the chapel was cool, the stained-glass windows tempering the straightforward brilliance of the spring light. The tableau of the Passion, displayed all around him, he hated. He could see no connection between the ninety minutes re-enactment of Christ on the cross 2,000 years ago and the rising sun over the Ayrshire fields, or with him on this Irvine afternoon of 1973 in Ayrshire, Scotland, and all the planets and galaxies extending out forever around this one centre among infinities of other centres, a centre because his being made it so.

★

He did not know exactly when his lust for taking birds' eggs was overtaken by his guilt, but it was around then. There was a night when his mother's face, pressed to the dark kitchen window after knocking when she came back one night from Bingo, as a kind of joke, white and grotesque in the electric light, so unsettled him that a few hours later he destroyed his collection in a fit of grief, smashing them all, crumbling the perfect patterned ellipses among their sawdust into fragments all mixed together, all their particularities and the circumstances of each egg's finding, every tree climbed, every gorse bush inspected from below, his head tilted up against the light for the telltale dark obstruction, melded into one, which was his guilt. He vaguely knew that he was not supposed to have such things anyway, that somewhere old men had said it was not allowed and that he could never show them to anyone or tell anyone about them; that the inexpressible loveliness of those eggs and the strange emotions they had stirred in him as his gaze gentled them in their cheap cardboard box was forbidden. That beauty had to be destroyed. It was not for the likes of him.

He could not even risk giving the collection to a museum, had he known how to do such a thing. One of his Observer's Books said that taking birds' eggs had been illegal since 1954. He would have had to tell them his dad or granddad had given them to him, and he couldn't take the risk. All over the country these small gatherings of air-light eggshells patterned and variously coloured were probably being crumbled into dust for similar reasons, and the evidence destroyed. All that still beauty in dark boxes like a dirty secret. They were all murderers and he was a murderer too. His mother's face, pressed against the dark window, laughing at the joke. The great unwritten story, locked in the vaults of shame and illegality, of birdnesting youths in the twenty years between 1954 and the early seventies, unconfessable to, even then. Many years later, far in his future, he would watch the opprobrium that greeted even nature celebrities such as David Attenborough and Chris Packham on their admission that collecting birds' eggs, even in a small way, had helped engender their interest in the natural world as boys. He saw a clip between a famous TV presenter and the ornithologist Bill Oddie during which the latter admitted to stealing—collecting—birds' eggs up till the age of ten, before 1954. 'But it was legal, then,' the presenter interjected immediately, desperate to preserve the respectability of her interviewee. As if that made any moral difference. They were all murderers; *Homo sapiens* was a murderous species. And perhaps even interest itself was a form of harm. It seemed illogical to think that a stroke of a pen in a high place legislating for the grubbing out of hedgerows or the use of a particular pesticide could affect, say, Britain's peewits or sparrowhawks more than a bunch of collecting schoolboys; nevertheless, it seemed so.

*

After that, something shifted in him. He still found nests and eggs, for which he seemed to have a special skill, but the idea of taking one, even of the commoner species, began to horrify him. Even eggs of birds that, a year or two earlier, would have seemed as exotic and valuable to him as the Koh-i-Noor diamond he left untouched and undisturbed.

PLATE 9.

Stewart delt   Lizars sc

SPARROW HAWK
Male & Female

Persistent collectors must be like thieves of rare and famous artworks who can't show the objects of their desire to anyone, so heavy is the weight of disapproval. Such collectors are literally possessed but unable to be illuminated in the light of others' regard; the desire corrupting in them like the picture of Dorian Gray in the attic.

And things developed in him. It had begun, strangely, in that first winter in Scotland when out one November morning he had seen a great white bird perched in the trees across the valley in the cold winter sunlight. A heron, though he did not know that then, caught in the light, shining with atypical whiteness. Then next was a small mousy brown bird ascending with little jerks up a tree trunk, flitting to the bottom of the next tree, ascending again, sometimes going up around the trunk in a spiral. A treecreeper.

His mother's catalogue became a source of more than occasional poring over the women's underwear section with its lacy pants and bras in pink, white, blue, and tangerine (as various as the brighter colours of the shells he had been possessed by), sometimes with their thrilling shadows of dark triangle, so subtle he was barely sure whether they were there or not. He began to find a strange satisfaction beyond that, of leafing through other pages of this thick, heavy volume, so lavishly illustrated with the objects of this world, all marked with an identifying letter, with the all-important prices beneath: how much you would pay if you could buy something outright, how much it would cost if you paid it up every week for 26 weeks, or for 52.

An uncle had given him a cheap telescope that, he soon learned, was almost entirely useless for even finding birds to look at in its dim, shaking little circle of gray light. The circle and the small flitting object he was trying to look at were difficult to align in all the space and twigs and branches round about— it was like searching for a particular sandgrain on a beach. What he needed, the Freemans' catalogue told him, were binoculars. He spent a long time going through its pages of glossy dark visual aids and reading the little descriptions. They seemed to promise an ideal world realised, though they required what he did not have: a form of magic. Money.

Sometime before, a school pal, 'Chip', so nicknamed because his straight thick hair was so greasy that a day after washing it would shine again with oils as if slicked with Brylcreem, had said: 'Fancy comin caddyin, Jed?' There was much interest in golf in some of the boys at Irvine Royal. One of the boys' fathers was the caddymaster at Western Gailes golf club, which seemed to give the boy some special status. Jed never took to the sport as such—golf for him was associated with middle-class things that had nothing to do with him. But Chip said: 'Twa pun a round fer caddyin. You comin?'

So one Saturday morning early at the caravan site's lane-end he got the green bus Chip also got on at, at Irvine Cross, for the Western Gailes. The bus dropped them off at the end of the lane up to the clubhouse. Here, every weekend morning, a bunch of money-hungry teenage boys would sit on the white wall outside the clubhouse in a row, watching while the golfers arrived with their bags and, a little after, the boy-with-status's father, from behind the wide glass window, would indicate with a pointing gesture which pair of boys he was choosing for a particular set of 'bags' which had just come in. Each boy, to make sure he was the one chosen, and not one sitting either side of him, would point to himself; the caddymaster would nod and the boy would walk jauntily across the crunching gravel to the clubhouse to pick up his bag. You were paid two pounds for a round which took three hours. Sometimes boys got more money if they knew about golf and could interact with the golfer. He heard of ranges of elite caddies for well-known golfers who could be paid a Croesian £30 for a round. For caddying had its range of hierarchies like everything else. He himself, though, was useless, just wanted the money so he could buy his binoculars to watch birds with, and never got more than the two pounds that was the standard going rate. The golfers would curse while each miniscule white ball through their ineptitude vanished unfindably into rough patches of tussocky grass. It was, Jed realised, sometimes his job to 'follow the ball' which, because it wasn't a finch or a lark, he had little interest in doing. He would find himself inexplicably to blame for his golfer's misstroke. 'Caddy lost the ball,' one golfer once muttered red-facedly, after a half-hour search for the small white stippled planet in the long grass.

The Western Gailes looked out onto the Firth of Clyde. What were those great white birds arrowing down suddenly into the water, with a vertical splash of white when they entered it, far out in the gray sea of a gray March Saturday? How did he find out they were gannets, solan geese, *Sula bassana*? There was no one there to tell him. But find out, somehow, he did.

He had to be paid a minimum of two pounds a round, no matter how inept he was as a caddy. Depending on how long it took that morning to 'get a bag', he could be waiting on the bus back to Cunninghamhead by 2pm, but sometimes it was 5pm. He would have a hot Scotch pie from the clubhouse as a treat: the hot grey meat, and the pastry packed with its lards, and the raised rim of crust around the pie for breaking off and eating separately in your fingers, and the pooling grease from the pie turning the paper of the white bag you were given it in semi-translucent. The steam from the pie rising in the cold air in the big space of the maritime afternoon with far gannets spearing into the Firth, making their distant splashes. Sometimes it was easy getting selected for a bag if not many boys were out; on one or two such memorable occasions, if you had the stomach for it, you might sit on the wall after a first round to see if you could get chosen again. Jed always had the stomach for it. He wanted those binoculars. After the cost of the pie was taken off, and the bus fare, he would get back to the caravan site at least a pound closer to his goal.

He got to know the optics section of the Freeman's catalogue pretty well over the weeks while he was saving. There were the most expensive pairs that he wanted most of course—he always had an eye for quality in things that were important to him—but

PLATE 21

THE SOLAN GOOSE
Young & Old Plumage.

they cost hundreds of pounds. He scrutinised the brief descriptions of each pair, probably made up by some weary copywriter frailly attempting to make each sound unique and interesting, as closely as if it was a poem or one of the descriptions in his two Observers' books. One pair especially, that came in at a reasonable £15.99, were described as 'ideal for watching wildlife'. They were a pair of Pathescope de Luxe 16x50s, among the most powerful magnification-wise in the catalogue pages, but also one of the cheapest. That should have alerted him but it didn't. They were what he could afford. *Ideal for watching wildlife...* He could see himself along the railway line, say, getting privileged glimpses into the lives of deer, or hares, or hovering kestrels, or who knows what. He told his mum he wanted to buy them.

—How will you pay for them? she said.

—I've got eight pounds already from caddyin.

So they were ordered. He waited expectantly. They arrived about a week later. They were heavy, big, and hung like a deadweight around his neck, and when he raised them to his eyes the image they showed was gray and dim. They magnified sixteen times, so they also magnified sixteen times the vibration in his hands as he held them to his eyes. The world was a thing of tremblings through their lenses. But they were a start, and for a little while he was happy. This big set of cheap optics were a first key into an entirely different world. Specks on boughs became recognisable creatures of beak and feather. He peered and squinted through their non-ideal lenses into another dimension, escaped along a road of light, however dim, into a fabulous imagined existence full of sightings of hawks and eagles and goldfinches and redpolls, a perfect world where nothing in it cared what he was doing when he made his furtive way across the car park to the entrance of St Mary's chapel.

The other boy on the site, in competition, got a pair of binoculars. His were small, old, solid, with the black oxidised off the edges of the lens barrels where you gripped them which showed the heavy brass they were made of below.

—They're ex-military, the boy told him. Ma da got them for me.

—Can I look?

They compared the two: Jed with his enormous Pathescopes de Luxe—the 'de Luxe' was a nice touch—and the other with his small, worn, solid Barr & Stroud binoculars. Jed examined these, at first, snootily. The smaller set only magnified six times. They were lighter, though, and when he raised them to his eyes he was astonished. The world through them was bright, luminous in fact, extraordinarily detailed, and it held still, more or less, like the world when he looked at it unaided. There were crosshairs—reticules, from the Latin, *reticulum*, 'little net'— in the centre of the bright round circle of light they made. He swung them to a crow on a bough and could see every feather.

—It's really sharp, he said.

—Aye, said the boy. Ma da says it's because they're ex-military and whatever's ex-military's ayewis the best. It hus tae be.

GOLDEN EAGLE

PLATE 12

This made sense to him and imbued these little Barr & Stroud 6x30s with a strange glamour. They had been used for tracking warships, or tanks, or soldiers moving in the woods. Now they were being used for watching crows on treetops, or distant kestrels, or grey wagtails on a river. He coveted them, experiencing the sense for perhaps the first time of an object being completely fit for purpose, as his massive Pathescope de Luxe binoculars were not. He wanted whatever he did or owned in this new interest to be perfect. The other boy lost interest soon enough. His was not a real interest but driven by a small sense of competition. He quickly moved onto other things.

6x30s. Jed went back to his mother's catalogue, and looked again with this new knowledge. There were no 6x30s, but there was a pair of 8x30s, made by Zeiss Zena Jenoptem, that looked similar to the Barr & Stroud binoculars of the other boy. But they were £24.99! He managed to sell his first pair to a cousin in Bellshill as 'excellent for watching wildlife' for £10. This he did without a qualm. It gave him about three pounds to start paying the others with. He remembered the gray November day they arrived. It was a Friday, and for some reason the school was closed early. He remembered the brilliance of the grey light in the lenses when he raised them to his eyes, as good as the Barr & Stroud binoculars, and lighter but solid in his hands. Then he could settle, as he had the right tool for the thing intended. He loved the precision of them. He loved the sharpness of the birds in the circle of light surrounded by darkness. He could be out there, through that circle, in that other world. It took his attention away from him and he was lost, and found, in some other universe where those other things—was that a redpoll? There was a dipper on the Lugton Water!—were what mattered, and his self-absorption and forgetfulness were a kind of bliss, though an inhuman bliss, beyond the unmanageable writhing turmoil of emotions.

It was around this time as part of this he became interested in the Latin names of birds. The names, in their strangeness and difference and seeming exactness, formed part of an ordered universe of light that kept manageable Janet Donaldson's terrifying, aweing white semi-translucent blouse and glimpse of starling-egg blue that if it got too near him threatened to incinerate his brain cells. *Coccothraustes coccothraustes, Fringilla coelebs, Fulmaris glacialis, Certhia familiaris, Ardea cinerea*....these, recited inwardly, were a litany holding at bay the great chaos and uncertainty of what talking to such a goddess might mean. And did you know the fulmar has the longest incubation period of any British bird at 52, 53 days? Did you know that tawny owl's eggs were spherical, like ping-pong balls, because the owls nested in tree holes where there was no danger of the eggs rolling out so they didn't need to be oval? Or that the long-tailed tit's nest could have up to 2,000 feathers for its lining (as they thought, then)?

He did not wonder with what expression of open-mouthed joy Janet Donaldson would receive these astonishing facts, breathlessly repeated from

PLATE 2

WATER OUZEL

PLATE 15.

HAWFINCH.

Stewart delt.

his remarkable memory. He could guess enough to know he would be met with scorn, pity and ridicule. His ideal woman would have been a Janet Donaldson who, improbably, had a huge obsessive interest in ornithology and knew already what a woodcock was—or at least was interested in finding out. But such a woman, if that paragon could ever exist, he thought, certainly didn't at Irvine Royal in the 1970s, or at least he never met her. He was on his planet. The girls were on theirs. His was filled with birds, birds' eggs, Latin names, owl pellets, herons' pectinated claws. He did not know what theirs was filled with. Their planet was remote and in another part of the universe. But he could be certain it would involve laughter and mockery at his own strangeness and flare-faced awkwardness. It was the beginning of the pain of isolation and the attempt to broach it, to find correspondences in another.

The arrival of the 8x30s Zeiss Jena Jenoptems marked the opening out of his whole world and his interest in birds. Thoughts in the head and the engineering brilliance and optical obsessions of numerous past geniuses were materialised in the little example of German craftsmanship he carried, swinging on their lanyard around his neck; sometimes, if he wasn't in active birdwatching mode, keeping them under his pullover to stop them penduluming or bouncing against his breastbone as they were prone to do in reaction to his long, loping strides. There they protruded like an odd, misshappen bust. They were the magic key; they were his

BLUE TITMOUSE.

secret ticket. Without them, everything would have
been different. He would, if he had thought about it,
have thanked in his mind effusively those makers and
obsessives whose lives and thoughts meant he could
tick a box in his mother's catalogue and a man called
a postman delivered a package for him at his fam-

ily's caravan door. Those makers were the kindling, the sticks, the coal. His fascination and impulse was the small flame of the match. Together they made a manageable fire he could warm himself at for the winter. Such things, had they a memory, could have stored, those small, solid optics, a grey wagtail in spring sunlight on the Annick Water, leaping into the air from a boulder of rich moss of the greenest green, twisting in the air after flies, alighting again on the boulder among wet shining and the rillings of water: the quick, repeated bobbing of the long tail, the sulphur yellow of its breast, the deep blue-gray, the colour of roof slates after rain, of its back. Or those far birds taking to the air with drawn-out, single, melancholy cries, just silhouetted, whose long decurved beaks identified them as curloos, and his amazement that such a creature could exist out there in the world and that he was allowed to see it. Or the moorhen that would skulk below flood-exposed tree roots and the fresh green overhanging leaves of wood club-rush on the opposite side of the Annick water: if he was careful he could sneak up, hidden by the opposite bank, and lie, comfortably enough on his belly, and watch in the shining spring light while this odd bird, with its waxy yellow and red bill, emerged to walk along below the bank, its tail 'ticking' up and down in synchrony with its slow, deliberated steps, the whole scene a small tableau of light and colour and focused detail. It was all shine and primary colour reflecting tinily on his irises.

He soon found that the little Observer's books of birds and birds' eggs were not enough to satisfy

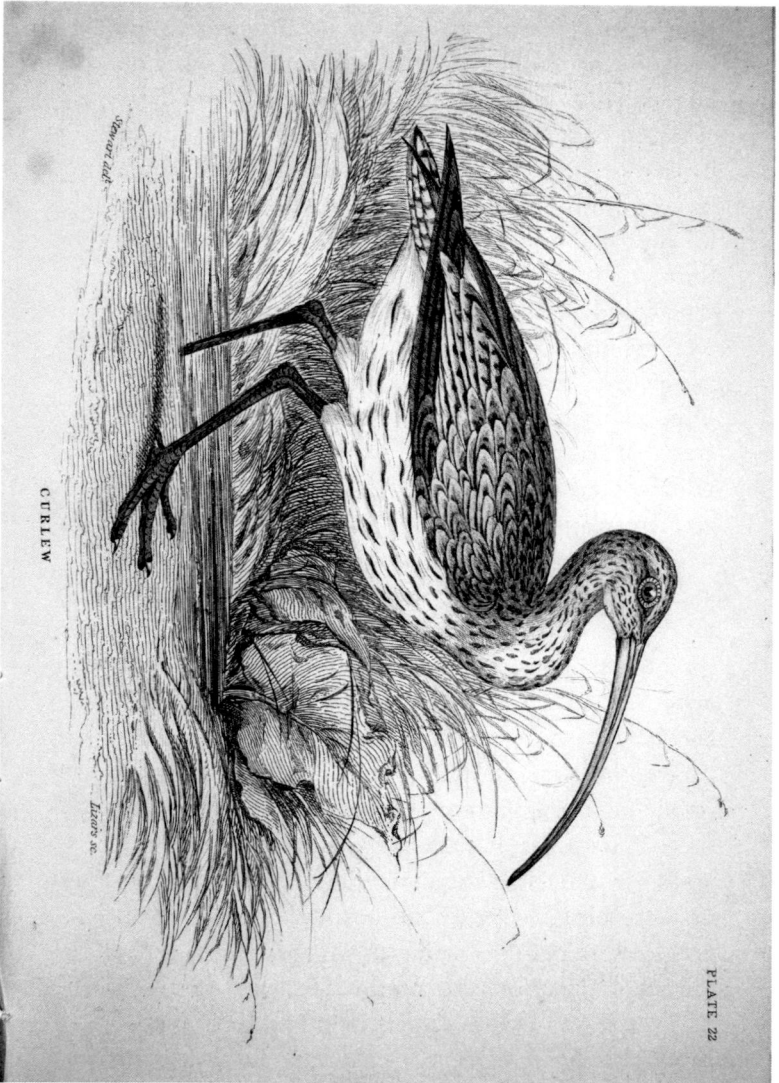

CURLEW

PLATE 22

his growing curiosity. One day in a bookshop in Kilmarnock, Justin Theodas's, he discovered the book he had to have. It was a hardback, heavy, large format volume, the *AA/Reader's Digest Book of British Birds*. He flicked through it. Not only did it have sizeable colour plates of all the birds which it covered; there were more details about the birds in their individual entries, along with a little map for each in the UK, showing in keyed colours where each could be found, and at what season. And there were whole sections on birds' eggs, migration, birds and people, finishing with a series of pages of maps of good places to see birds—even including his own area! He actually lived in a 'real' place that 'they'— whoever made books—could put on a map. This was a revelation to him.

There was only one problem. The book cost £4.15, which he did not have. He went back to caddying and for a few weeks, every time he visited the bookshop to check with thudding heart if the book was still there, it was. Finally he bought it, and another world opened to him. This volume was his centre, the bird oracle he could consult if he needed to find out something. If not all, at least a lot of it was there in its pages. It even had a section on choosing good binoculars. He would read entries about two or three bird species every morning, between 8am and 8.20am, before starting down the long lane for the school bus: focusing on the words almost like a litany, the way a religious fanatic might focus on the Bible. It formed an important part of his day. If he could not have this space, for whatever reason, at the start of the day, he was unsettled for the rest of it.

His father did not like him but his mother did, and her presence acted to deflect some of his father's hostility and resentment. In his head he saw her as the saintly nurturer and his father as the gruff, grudging and truculent presence to whom he was unwelcome and disturbing. When his mother was there, like an animal he could eat whatever he wished; when she was not, his presence in the kitchen making a sandwich or whatever else would be watched over by his father so that he did not take too much cheese on bread, for instance; a second cup of tea might provoke a comment. It was made clear to him that the food he took was not his own to eat as much of as he wanted. It was being paid for, he was not paying for it, and at some point he would be. It was difficult to understand when this had all started, but he didn't feel he was entirely without fault. Once as a little boy he had been taken to some sort of variety performance: a musical affair, full of razzamatazz, glary brilliance, and singing. Coming down the busy stairs afterwards his father, plainly animated and pleased, and confident of agreement, had said, 'Well, did you like that then?' He had. He had liked it despite himself. But something about his father's childlike pleasure and confidence of agreement made him say the opposite.

—No. No.

Far away, instantly, inside his father, he had seen the shutters drop on a little bit of light shining out towards him and his father's recoil as those two syllables hit. He was seven, or perhaps eight. So his father now disliked him and he did not blame him for that. It only meant that, all those years later, he was not welcome. Where did the 'no' come from? Was it a desire to reject what he had been given as somehow not good enough, to differentiate himself from that, even at a young age, to seek something else? As a wee boy there had been something in him that had hated dailiness and ordinariness as not serious enough, by his own lights. Or, rather, it was as if he felt unmoored and cast adrift and given to chaos if he was not doing something that engaged him. He was wasting time, and time was wasting him.

Now what it had come to was that at every opportunity he escaped, whatever the weather and season, outdoors. If his mother was absent, the harshest weather or season were kinder than the caravan on the site on top of the hill where his father brooded like a dragon over the gold hoard which was his wife's attention and affection.

★

So it was, on mornings he escaped school, Saturdays and Sundays and holidays, he developed a routine. Saturdays were his favourite. His parents' bedroom was at the other end of the caravan, and they had a lie-in on Saturdays. His sisters' bedroom— they slept in bunk beds—was the same size as his and it abutted the kitchen where sometimes his father's penchant for late night fry-ups would wake and unsettle him. His head lay just through the wall where the cooker was. His father for some inexplicable reason had replaced the bedroom doors,

PLATE 8.

Stewart delt.   Lizars sc.

FIRE CROWNED & COMMON GOLD-CREST.

which used to close snugly like normal doors, with doors on runners, that left an unusually large gap at the door edge even when closed. Light flooded in if anyone turned the light on in the kitchen. He would lie there miserably, assailed by the sizzle and reek of frying chips at 11.30pm, in the little room in whose short single bed he had to lie, slightly curled, like a foetus, enduring the clatter and animal-like activity of his father late on a Friday night when he had no work to go to the following morning. They were all animals, really. Occasionally Jed would say something to indicate that the palaver had woken him, but it did not matter. He had no power. Then the sizzling sound would stop, there would be the scraping of the chips emptied out onto a plate, the kettle making its gradually increasing rushing sound of heat-agitated water would click off, there'd be the clink-clink-clink of a stirring teaspoon, and the light would flick off, returning his bedroom to sweet concealing darkness. He could try to sleep again.

But Saturday mornings were his favourite. He would be up early in the morning silence with the whole family sleeping round about, able to eat whatever he wanted without his father's scrutiny; his sisters steadily breathed in their bedroom; his foster-brother stayed with an uncle in a small, adjacent caravan. Cheese sandwiches for breakfast, the cheddar in thick orange slabs, the sliced bread white and soft. He would eat it slowly, to taste each mouthful properly. And what he liked in the silence was the anticipation about the day ahead. He might see anything. He did not know. Usually, if he thought enough about it in advance, he would bring extra cheese sandwiches and perhaps some biscuits, in a little green canvas shoulder bag. Then, sometimes at the first sign of any stirring from the others, he would go. Oh these Saturday mornings, when the world was an unwritten page or an unfootstepped field of snow, or a great clear space under the sky, a thing of distances he could walk into and be lost in! Often he would be gone for the whole day, taking whatever direction would suit him or took his whim. He had no maps, only his impulses. When he got back, many hours later, ravenous, if he was lucky his mother would be there to cook him his tea or be a point of shelter. If he was unlucky he would forage for himself, watched over. Like a hawk mantling he would take whatever he'd been able to make into the refuge of his bedroom, his one sacrosanct area in the caravan, which was his territory. It was small, but it was his. A little window at the far end, set in the end of the caravan, gave a view of the next caravan over, aligned in the same direction as theirs, with the site wall beyond it and, visible above and beyond it, the woods across the river in the direction of Fairliecrevoch and, above that, if the weather was fair, the high blue and its white cloudlets diminishing into the distance.

It was around this time he became especially interested in owls. He was certain there was a tawny owl—he could hear it—in the witchwood across the river. Then one day—the 12 September 1973, which he remembered exactly because it was the day he started keeping a nature notebook in a blue hardback—he had stepped into the wood edge and, at the foot of a Scots Pine, in the needles, was a pellet—a cylinder of fur, glutinous, wet-fresh, still with specks of what must have been, he thought, owl saliva. He bent to it, astonished. He had read about owl pellets. Owls swallowed their prey whole, at a gulp, they did not pick and choose the choicest bits, like a man delicately removing the thick reams of fat from a steak with a knife and fork. Down it went, the mouse, the vole, the shrew, in a gulp into the owl's stomach, and whatever it could not digest, the bones, the little scaly feet and tail, the fur, it brought back up as a pellet. There was an owl in the witchwood! He cupped the cold soddenness of the pellet in his palm, stood up, and looked at the tree branches above him—and from several feet above his head, with a single sideways step along a branch, a tawny owl, big, round-headed, launched itself thrillingly off into the air in all its brown-barred feathered and mothy-winged magnificence, and winged silently away through the trees, to a sudden commotion and clatter, far off, among the small birds, their exclamations and ticking and chinking protests marking the owl's unseen progress through the wood. He simply stared after it in amazement. An owl! A real, live, wild, owl! It was his, though it wasn't his. But he was the only person to see it, perhaps the only person who ever would see it. What was amazing about it, apart from the beauty of its feather patterns and the big, rounded wingtips, and its way of flying, with quick beats yet also, as if, strangely, in slow motion, was the flight's sheer silence.

PLATE 28

TAWNY OWL.

Exhilarated, he took the pellet carefully home to his bedroom.

—D'you have tweezers and a needle? he asked his mum.

—What are you lookin them for?

—Oh, just an experiment.

On a sheet of white paper, he teased the pellet apart. It held little skulls, other small unidentifiable bones, the jawbone of what, with its curved pointed tooth, he later identified as a shrew's, and the black wing cases of a small beetle. The jawbone he drew and labelled carefully in his blue notebook. This had been, like the rest of the pellet, in the stomach of the owl that had flown away through the trees.

In the weeks and months afterwards he became an owl detective, trying to trace its movements. He read up about owls, how their ears were hidden behind

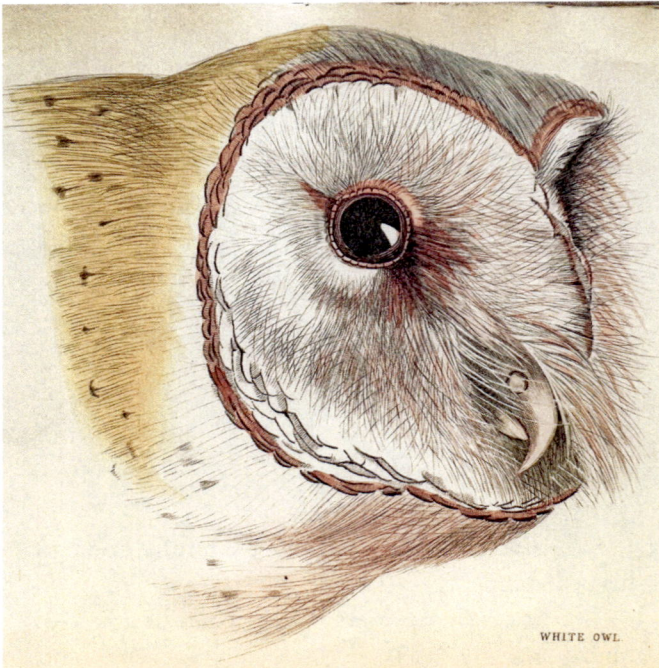

WHITE OWL.

their facial disks and placed asymmetrically so there was a timelag in the same sound reaching each ear so they could locate its direction more easily. He read that the Barn Owl for instance could catch a mouse in complete darkness by hearing alone. He read about their specially designed—evolved—feathers, softer than other birds' so they could fly silently.

He would try tracking the owl in the wood. It left, like teasing signs, indications of its presence in the form of dropped feathers, usually the smaller, slightly wispier breast feathers, which he could identify by comparing them to the amazing detail in the plates, by Raymond Harris Ching, of the bird paintings in the *AA Book of British Birds*. Once he found a primary feather from its wing: a remarkable item, buff and with various shades of brown, boldly barred with markings the colour of milk chocolate. But what was amazing about it was its softness: the surface had a furriness to it as if it was halfway between a bird and, say, the velveteen of the coat of a mole. He carried this back like some religious object, holding it carefully by the keratin quill, to his bedroom where it joined the growing collection of feathers and miniature skulls, like a small altar for worshipping an unknown god, on the top of his small chest of drawers below the bedroom window.

It was many months later that he discovered the giveaway pile of pellets below a sitka spruce near the edge of the wood, indicating the owl's regular roost. There it was, high up, sitting against the trunk, its body drawn up vertically so it would better blend in and be camouflaged, in the intimate bright circle of

the binoculars, the scene edged with the dry spiki-
ness of spruce twigs. This stance, he would later
read, was called its 'attenuated posture'—a way of
trying to camouflage itself when it might be discovered during the day. He would often pick his
way carefully, taking care not to crack any twigs,
to stand near the base of the tree and see through
binoculars if the bird was there. And often it was,
its body stretched vertically. These encounters were
a small point of connection between the bird and
himself; entirely silent, and secret.

He learned, one day, to hoot like an owl, cup-
ping his hands together and making an airtight cav-
ern within them. He would put his lips to his paired
thumbs, covering the knuckle joints, and blow
into them. The air would escape from the slit left
below the base of his thumbs and it was this that
made the sound. Where had he got the idea for this?
He couldn't remember. Perhaps one of the boys at
school had been shown it by his father, like generations of other boys before him. All he knew was that
he had spent a whole day obsessively trying to coax
sound from his hands, and that the sound, when it
finally emerged, if you blew gently, if you got the
knack right, was rich and mellow and sonorous. It
was a form of magic.

On winter nights of frost, when things were
particularly bad with his father, he couldn't watch
TV. When Jed sat at the end of the couch, to stop him
seeing the screen his father would rest his right fist
against his waist so his elbow jutted out and blocked
the view. The teenager would take a torch and go

PLATE 31

Stewart del.

LONG EARED OWL.

crunching off across the fields in the exhilarating
cold towards Annick Lodge. The owls were calling
out there under constellations. He would swing the
torch beam silently in a glide and a swoop with an
imperious whimsy across the dark sky above his
head, seeing the beam simply disappear at the limit

of its earthly power. And he would climb the yews
near the big white stone gateposts at the entry to
the estate drive and hoot to the owls, occasionally
strafed by the glary brilliant headlights of a passing
car: to the drivers a figure, could they have seen him,
like a kind of owl himself.

★

What was he in the school? Awkward, bumbling,
silent often. If he arrived at a classroom for a lesson with the huge stuffed satchel he carried under
one arm as the straps had broken under the weight
of books and jotters, and there was a bunch of girls
standing outside the class in a little huddle—the
horror!—he would stand and examine with exag-
gerated interest the most inane posters on the class
notice board in the corridor. He didn't seem able to
talk to a girl, and the more she attracted him the less
able was he to open his mouth. He dealt with the
problem of lunchtimes, as he dealt with most other
problems, with a ritual: he left the school and walked
up the High Street to the library in the townhouse
where he spent 45 minutes each day, poring over the
small nature sections. Ludicrous and long-forgotten
books engaged him: *But Hibou was Special*, about
a family's pet owl; or books detailing scenarios of
coming ecological disaster. The light of spring, bare
and strangely savage, poured out of the sky above
the Firth of Clyde and prised open with light the
grimacing faces in the streets of the little town.

He was old enough now not to go with his family

to Mass. Instead, on Sunday mornings, under pretence of going, he would take his bicycle and ride down the lane as if he was cycling into Irvine for chapel. But at Middleton Farm he would turn right and take the small B-road that led down past the white gateposts at the entrance to Annick Lodge. The big house at the end of its gravel driveway was set among mature broadleaved trees and was invisible from the road. He would freewheel past this and down the slope to the Pier Brae where the Annick Water flowed past, trickling musically, below a small bridge; put the lock around his bike behind trees on the riverbank, and walk along it among the trees for an hour or more. After a plausible period had passed he would retrace his steps, cycle up the brae, and then back up the long drive to the caravan site, finally free that day after having created the illusion for his mother that he had been to Mass. He disliked this pretence; that, for these two hours on a Sunday morning, his time was not his own, but it got rid of the problem of his being revealed at Irvine Royal as a Catholic.

—Who said Mass today? asked his mum.

—Father O'Connell.

—What was his sermon about?

—Oh, just about being kind to others and not telling lies.

The ludicrous banality of this was sufficiently plausible, it seemed, to convince his mother. It was not worth taking a stand and telling her the real reason why he was not going to Mass. It would have meant talking about the rampant sectarianism that he felt was nothing to do with him. This small lie was easier and, he gauged, probably less harmful in the long run.

Only once did his subterfuge come close to being revealed, when Margaret, a neighbour, came over to his mother's and sat in the little kitchen and sipped coffee. She contradicted his version, given earlier, of which priest had taken Mass.

—Margaret says it was Father Donaghy took Mass, not Father O'Connell this morning.

—Well, one of them, he said. Sometimes I forget which is which. This also sounded plausible.

—And she says his sermon was about World War Three, not about friendship, his mother went on.

—He probably wasn't listening very hard, said Margaret, laughing. She had a very kind, light, and what he interpreted as a teasingly flirtatious, manner.

—His mind was on other things, like birds, she said.

It was as if she was laughing at him but not unkindly. She sat in her snug sweater that was the pale blue of a starling's egg. She was kind to him and he could sin with her in imagination.

He sinned often and with varying degrees of contrition. No one told him what he would later understand, that in his attempts at holiness and purity he was pitting his tiny moral impulse against the huge and unstoppable force of biology, like opposing an untutored and untrained farmboy against the warrior Achilles, and that he could only lose. He sinned in the landscape, lying among coppices of hazel, deep in beds of crushed wildflowers, splashing the fields and woods of Ayrshire, but more usually in bed at night. The aftermath was relief and guilt. Sometimes he could manage without sinning for several days and so feel better about himself. If he managed it for a week, which was about his limit in usual circumstances, he felt as holy as a priest or a monk; the world was a thing of shining light, built in barren splendour. But then some glimpse or gesture or the way Margaret had talked to him as she stepped off the bus at the lane-end entered that shining holy space and, lush and sharp-smelling as the nettles in the June ditches, goblin things of hair and laughter coaxed him back to sin. In thirty seconds the world he had so carefully constructed, piece by piece in the previous week, had toppled at a spurt, like some huge tower of sand or ash collapsed at the brush of a fingertip. The following day he would blush more easily again at school, no longer defended. He hated how his acts showed in his face.

—He's goat a beamer! He's goat a riddie! the boys would shout out at school around any of their unfortunate friends who had the beginnings of a blush at something that had been said. Round they would then gather, all warming their hands at this imaginary fire the blusher's embarrassment had kindled; the faint glow turned into a raging conflagration. 'Beamer! Riddie!' It was a peculiar form of agony and humiliation. The victim would be left twisting and turning and writhing. How red could a face get? How long could a humiliation last? —till the group's attention had moved somewhere else like a squall across a landscape; the victim's radiant cheeks would slowly fade back to normality, like the winter fire in the stove in his caravan slowly settling. If there were girls there also witnessing this ritual it made it worse of course as girls, in their white blouses and their striped school ties, astonishing as birds' eggs cored with red-lightninged yolk and albumen, were the hapless instigators of all that inconvenient, face-pulping blood.

A boy whose father was a public figure in the town showed a bunch of them, one lunchtime, a black-and-white magazine that had come he said from Denmark. The little group of spotty boys leafed through its pages with slightly affected expressions of astonishment. Why was this woman looking so happy to have her face so splashed? Did women do that? Did they like that? Was that how it happened? He looked, like the rest of the boys, at the images but felt strangely untouched and unaffected by them, as much as if they were pictures of animals in a zoo. Was that what the girl who wore the white polo-neck sweater, with sometimes a few spots on her face—purity and sinning combined—that he liked, wanted? Not that he would ever find out. If he could say even a brief sentence to her he felt as if he'd climbed to the topmost branches of a really difficult tree.

He thought that a way to get girls to like him would be to be powerful and strong. That was what girls wanted, wasn't it? His body was already changing. Hair began growing on unexpected parts of it. A strip of hair began to appear under his chin along one side of his Adam's Apple in a thin furze.

He was proud of this small wisp of transmutation
as it darkened and grew thicker, followed by hair
elsewhere—'bumfluff' the boys all called it—along
his jawline. He had no idea how to shave. His father
didn't talk to him now except for the slightest grunts
of disapproval or to say something forbidding. His
mother bought him shaving foam and a razor. He
wetted his face, applied the foam, scraped it along
his jawline, shearing the pus-filled tops of the few
spots along his chin in a mix of foam and blood,
wincingly, and rinsed it all off. The skin was left red
and tender and soft and sore, stinging sharply when
he splashed, as you were supposed to do, aftershave
lotion on it. This was his body. New crops of spots
began appearing, to his shame and embarrassment.
They were the sign to the world that he was a sinner,
an ordinary sinner like everybody else, and not the
holy example of light, unharnessed from the raging
animal body, that he aspired to. He felt for the first
time the weight of having a body, the unpredictable potential treachery of it. It was not him—as he
thought—but he was joined to it like some leering,
hairy, purulent, conjoined twin. Its fate was his fate,
one that he could not escape or control.

★

He had seen in newspapers adverts for the Charles
Atlas bodybuilding course. He sent away for the
promotional materials but, when they arrived,
Charles Atlas in the pictures was not very impressive.
To the young boy he looked like someone's

granddad who occasionally hoisted haybales at the weekend. It was plain he was, so to speak, on the way out. One day in some newspaper or other he saw another bodybuilding ad, this time for a course called, with either irony or optimism, *Hercules II*. He knew vaguely who Hercules had been. The promotional materials when they arrived did a hard sell on any male half-embarrassed by his physique. *Tired of being ignored by women? Tired of being passed over by the most beautiful girl in college?* (It was obviously aimed at American students, but he overlooked that bit.) 'College' could also translate to Irvine Royal. 'The most beautiful girl' could translate very easily to Gillian Witherspoon, whose redhaired ringletted friendliness he had begun noticing, imagining himself in some scenario walking the railway line, hand in hand, with her, to the strains of Donny Osmond's 'Puppy Love'. The man on the front cover of the main promotional booklet did look, vaguely suspiciously, as if someone had clipped his head from another photograph of a skinnier specimen, and attached it atop the full length, swimming-trunked, abdominally-rippling body of Hercules II below it, but such was the attraction to Jed of achieving such a physique himself at that point that his suspension of disbelief was almost total.

You too can have this body! Let me tell you my story. One year ago I too was a skinny non-entity. (Cue photographs of some head perched atop a skinny, white, almost emaciated frame.) *I was depressed. I felt life was passing me by. Then I decided to do something about it. Can you imagine what it would be like to have women casting*

admiring glances at your shoulders? (In a fantasy Tolk-
ienesque in its extravagance, Jed did imagine it.) The
materials went on to describe how the man in the
front cover photograph had transmuted himself in
several months from a pigeon-chested emaciated ex-
cuse for masculinity into the suave, confident, smiling, sauntering fielder of women's admiring awe-
struck glances. As a consequence he had invented the
life-changing course that, for just twelve pounds, he
would give you the secret to. *Imagine your woman delighted by your new physique! Imagine her running her fingers along your rippling biceps! No man or woman will ever
make fun of you again! Abraham Lincoln said, 'Walk softly
but carry a big stick.' With Hercules II, your physique is
your big stick.*

Jed was 14. He was credulous, then convinced. He
sent the little ad with the introductory payment of
two pounds though it involved first the humiliation
of having to approach his father to write him out a
cheque. It would have been much easier to deal with
his mother, but only his father had a chequebook.
His father made the most, emotionally, of this desire—which amounted to desperation in its intensity—on his son's part, and interrogated him for some
minutes. It was the most words they'd exchanged at
a time for many months.

—Who is it payable to?

—I don't know what you mean.

—Who should I make the cheque out to? Who
are you sending the money to?

—Oh. *Hercules II.* Write it out like that. He
handed him the slip of paper where he'd written the

second part out in roman numerals so there could be *no mistake.*

—*Hercules II?* His father got as much doubt and disdain into the words as he could.

—Yes.

—What is this for?

—It's a course I'm taking.

—A course.

—Yes.

—What sort of a course?

—A health course.

—A health course? What d'you want a health course for?

—To get healthy.

—Are you not healthy enough?

—I don't think I am.

He could hardly tell him, his pot-bellied, lager-swilling father, who drank six cans a night in front of the TV out of sheer unhappiness, that he was trying to transform himself into a shining Hercules so women would all admire him and no man—including his father—would dare to push him around ever again.

Finally, after various delays in signing the cheque, his father put his name to it and it could be slipped into the envelope with the clipped-out form and sent to the address Jed had, with great care, printed out by hand on the envelope in legible capitals. He had no idea how long it would take to reach London but having sent the form he settled into that privileged space that is the gap between setting some—potentially life-changing—event in motion and then having to carry it out. He bore it around with him, this secret knowledge of his coming transformation into Hercules. It was like a bright space in his mind that improved the possibilities of life after he had changed himself from his current state. In that new existence he moved, smiling and thoroughly capable, immense-shouldered and narrow-hipped, among admirers, as did Steve Reeves the famous filmstar bodybuilder whose photograph had appeared in the publicity materials for Hercules.

The first two parts of the course arrived—a day of high excitement—and thereafter, once he'd gone through the weekly angst and humiliation of handing over his pound and persuading his father to write the next instalment cheque—another part arrived every week for three months. It showed the exercises he would have to carry out to fulfil his dream, interspersed with inspiration stories and, throughout, illustrated by the strange photograph of the muscular torso with the author's head perched on top of it. He was not to exercise every day, Hercules advised. The body needed time between its workouts to recuperate and to build muscle.

And he was to increase his food intake substantially. The impressive list of what he should be consuming for breakfast every morning constituted a problem if his father, who policed his food intake, got wind of his new dietary requirements. These included such luxuries as orange juice, something the family never drank.

—Orange juice? said his mother when he asked her. You mean, diluting orange?

—No. It has to be real orange juice.

His mother looked worried. Diluting orange was one thing. Real orange juice was another matter. It was exotic.

—I'll see if they have it, his mother said.

Four times a week, after his family had gone to bed, and the caravan living room was free, he would start his workout—press ups, abdominal exercises, pull ups, which he managed with a length of stick he'd found and varnished as a sort of hiking accoutrement fully in accord with his having all the best items for any activities he cared about. This stick he positioned between two chair backs. If he positioned them correctly the chairs did not tip in towards him when he pulled himself up between them. These exercises he conducted in a late-night, heart-thudding tension between fulfilling his commitment to becoming Hercules and listening out in case the bumps and vibrations of his panting and straining would stir his father and the threat of his disapproval.

He began eating more heavily, as Hercules advised. This was much more than he would usually have eaten, but it was in the cause of building an impressive physique. Often he would take off his top and scrutinise himself in the mirror, from hour to hour, inspecting his torso for the slightest gain.

It was after several weeks of this that he noticed there was a problem. Hercules' shoulders remained, more or less, as they were, but he seemed to be putting weight on around his middle! All those power breakfasts had not in fact put on muscle but fat. This was the first time in his life he had been aware of any correlation between what he was eating and its effect on his physiology. Hercules, and his arrival among admirers, began to fade, sadly, into the distance. Now what had happened was that food, for the first time in his life, had become a *problem*, something he noticed. He began skipping lunch and went the whole day, from breakfast at eight till four-thirty when he got home from school, without eating. His visits to the library at lunchtime now became about reading diet books. He grew obsessed with healthy eating. In the library he discovered a book by Gayelord Hauser, an unlikelily named American proponent of healthy eating, friend to Hollywood film stars and other famous personages. His tales of eating fruit, whole grains and rice, all couched in a light, airy, conversational American style, Jed found strangely reassuring and consoling. What he now feared most, after his experience of putting *on* weight, was being *out of control*. No matter what, you could control what you put into your body via food. He determined that after his failed attempt—as it had turned out—to become Hercules II he could be, nonetheless, in control of his body. He began getting fussy about food. *This* was good; *that* was bad. Food, as Hercules II had been before it had revealed its hidden complications, was a form of magic, a way of changing how you looked. His mother grew alarmed and irritated by these changes in him. Feeding her son was ingrained deeply in her. Now he was refusing to be fed what had been perfectly acceptable before, rejecting it as not good enough; so she was not good enough. A strange new dynamic developed between them around food: his mother importuning him to eat something he stubbornly refused to eat. But it was through food, or rather the lack of it, he was discovering, that you could be light and airy, and your body could be like light, as little an encumbrance as possible. Food was how the outer became the inner, and was transformed to the outer again in the form of his body. It was made of sunlight and earth and water. He was striving for some kind of purity in a spring Ayrshire where the beeches in their resplendent soft fine lime all over the county were gently opening in a gauze, a haze of summer foliage where they could be seen for miles like a gesture of grace and beauty.

★

One morning in the late winter the whole class was given a sex-education lecture. He was skewered between fascination and terror of being seen to be fascinated, but the terror was greater than the fascination. He survived this double period by gazing straight ahead and not commenting to anyone else in any way, which would have immediately kindled in his face a beamer with all the potentially terrible consequences to follow. *He's got a riddie! Whit's he been daein?!* There was some brief mysterious point made about the importance of getting off at Paisley rather than going all the way to Glasgow. He was able to make it across the tightrope over the canyon of the hour and ten minutes by focusing on a neutral object. So he sat, like a man in an oilskin in the middle of a field, its hood up, head down while a torrent poured out of the whole sky over him and the water ran in rivulets down the hood and dripped into the grass. He knew that he was a sinner and that all it would have taken would be the slightest remark to start a chain reaction that would result in his humiliation, like a finger flicking a switch that would illuminate, out of the darkness, light by light, a whole city progressively out to the horizon. He was a Catholic and so was guilty for everything, by default. Once at another school at an assembly he had been sitting in the front rows and one of the teachers had launched into an irate diatribe about vandalism in the boys' toilets, extreme graffiti of a sexual nature. 'And make no mistake,' the teacher thundered, with conviction, 'we will find the culprit of these disgusting messages.' The teacher surveyed the assembled rows where, somewhere, the guilty party sat. For whatever reason, he caught his glance. In seconds he could feel it starting in his face, the beginning of a blush that, a minute later, had reached its full extent so he sat there helplessly, his face burning like a red coal in a field of snow. He was entirely innocent. But here was his body accusing him, as if it was taking on the guilt of the world.

It was only, in their sex-education lecture, when the teacher began talking about diseases that he was able to relax. These were terrible, just punishments for something that seemed to offer so much pleasure. He could understand why they existed. Photographs were shown. There was an especially terrifying one called syphilis, terrifying because it went 'underground' and could operate in your system for years till its final, deadly stage, like some horrible parasite eating away, deep down, at the structure of a house, invisibly, until one day the house collapsed irreparably. It began with a small sore called a 'chancre'. Somewhere, at the back of his mind, in the past he could not control as it had already happened, a small door opened onto a memory of a little spot he had had 'down there' at age eleven, the same summer they had had the scabies and the subterranean burrowing mites between their fingers and down there had had the whole family scratching incessantly at an itch that would not go away. He had at the time seen by chance in a red encyclopaedia a reference to a 'chancre', the first sign of syphilitic infection. He was eleven. The idea that this, on him, might be such a thing, given the maddening lack of detail in the description, had shadowed him at eleven for a few days. It was a proper punishment for the timeless few hours he and Sophie Buxton spent in the shed in a holy hush, among cobwebs and the whiff of creosote in front of an audience of leering paint tins that had now-solidified emulsion dribbled down their rusting chins. At the end of the lesson, as the pupils crowded chattering at the exit to the classroom, the distant memory of this, far back, opened its door in the back of his mind. *Chancre.*

It was lunchtime. He strode, in a state of increasing unease, up the High Street to the library in the townhouse. This time he ignored the natural history section and the nutrition section where Gayelord Hauser silently enthused about the joys of whole

grains and brown rice with Greta Garbo, the impli-
cation being that on such superfoods you would live
forever; he went direct to the medical section where,
among indexes, under 'S', he looked it up. *Chancre.
The initial sore that indicates the presence of syphilis. This
disease has three stages: primary (the chancre stage); secondary; tertiary. In the secondary stage the disease appears to be
dormant. This stage if untreated can last for many years,
and leads if untreated to the tertiary stage, which results in
madness, blindness, degenerating disease and finally death.
Treatment is easiest in the primary stage.*

He stared at these entries. Was that what he had
had when he was eleven? It was a punishment for his
sin. At this very moment the spirochaetes—micro-
scopic worms—that caused the final stages could be
nibbling away, somewhere deep inside him. There
was no one he could tell. There was only him, the
books, and his uncertain memory. He read the accounts again, scrutinising them and sifting them for
clues that would mean he could definitively rule it
out, but he couldn't. He tried to build a wall against
the thought in his mind, but the higher he built the
wall the taller and louder the demon grew behind it.

So he did something which was entirely alien to
him and in ordinary circumstances would never have
been something he'd have needed, this young person
who could climb to the tops of high trees with ease
and was at his happiest out gazing into the distance
through the bright lenses of binoculars, or vaulting
fences, having his forearms raked by brambles so the
blood came up in little speckles all along the gashes
as he tried to check whether, say, a longtailed tit's

nest had eggs, or returning exhausted from a day's wandering in whatever direction he had chosen. He made an appointment with the doctor, at a surgery in the High Street. This itself was an intimidating

PLATE 22

EUROPEAN NUTHATCH.

procedure: *which doctor did he wish to see?* He had no
idea, so he chose the first one offered, a Dr Burns.

The afternoon of his appointment, after school,
was a lyrical spring teatime full of new light. The
peewits and curloos were nesting up country. The
sweet cicely was opening its heavy-scented, intricate
umbels in the hedges that gave you a gust of their
perfume as you passed. Lords and Ladies were opening at the bottom of hedges and in gusty woods, un-
furling their rolled spikes to spathes, the lime green
hoods like the cowls of monks.

He sat in the awkward silence of the waiting
room, a silence made immeasurably more awkward
when Jennifer O'Halloran, a girl with a mass of au-
burn tumbling over her blazered shoulders, kindled
by the spring light, came in and sat. She gave him
a small flare of recognition and sat down, probably
thinking exactly what he was: *why are you here?*

A receptionist came out and called his name, with
a question mark at the end of it.

—Yes?

—Dr Burns will see you now.

He rose and entered the doctor's office. The clinical, sparkling accoutrements of medical enquiry;
stethoscope; rubber gloves.

The doctor was a balding older man with a kindly
manner.

—So what can we do for you? he said.

—Doctor, he blurted out, with a bluntness aided
by the fact that this was something he'd never told
another living soul. I think I have syphilis.

—Syphilis, eh? said the doctor.

—Yes.

—What makes you think that?

—I had a chancre.

—A chancre? Hmm.

—Yes.

—Where?

—On my... he had difficulty saying the actual word...on my...penis.

—On your penis, eh?

He winced a little as the word was repeated back to him.

—Yes.

—What did this chancre look like?

—It was a small red spot, down there.

—Where, exactly?

—Just at the tip.

—How long did it last? Is it there now?

—No, he said quickly, terrified in case he might have to show this strange man his penis. —I can't remember. Maybe a month?

—A month. Hmm. When was this?

—When I was eleven.

—Eleven. The way the doctor kept repeating everything back to him would have been annoying had he not been so desperate for absolution.

—How do you think you acquired this chancre? From a toilet seat?

—This introduced a new and terrifying possibility, hitherto unspeculated on, into the boy's head.

—Can you get them from toilet seats?

—No. But sometimes people imagine they can. So where?

—From a girl.

—A girl. How old was this girl?

—The same age as me. Eleven.

The doctor was barely able to conceal a chuckle now.

Jed's face flared into a roar of red blood.

—Look, the doctor said, collecting himself into his best serious manner. This is all highly unlikely.

—But I think that's what I've got doctor!

—Where did you find out about syphilis?

—At a sex-education lecture at school. Last week.

—Look, the doctor said, with a hint of annoyance. —I could send you to a Special Clinic where you could be seen by a specialist but I am reluctant to waste their time. It is highly unlikely you have syphilis. It is a disease of adults.

—But I'm worried, doctor!

—Go away and forget about it. The Special Clinic is for people who have real problems. There's nothing wrong with you. If you notice anything else, come back and see me, but I really don't think there is anything to worry about.

The auburn-headed girl resplendent in her white shirt, school tie a little loosened at the collar, and royal blue blazer, lit a little when he passed her on the way out. Oh why could he not be pure and perfect and able to talk to her! Instead he was diseased.

On the bus home, after perhaps twenty minutes of repeating to himself, '*It is highly unlikely. Disease of adults. There is nothing wrong with you,*' he knew with absolute conviction that he was dying and would not be long for this world. The doctor had said 'it is *highly* unlikely', but '*highly*' was not 'unlikely' enough. When there was the merest chink of darkness able to enter the perfect shining room he imagined for himself and his life he could not invest in making his future perfect. The spirochaetes could at that very moment be working underground, along his backbone and in his brain cells. How could the doctor know? The answer was that he couldn't. He wasn't a *great enough authority*. His leaving even a chink for the dark possibility to widen and enter in a full flood showed that he couldn't know. Jed needed complete certainty before he could commit himself to all he had to do. That night in bed he prayed, repeating the habitual words over and over. *Our Father, who art in heaven, hallowed be thy name…*

Two days later he was back in Dr Burns' consulting room.

—Doctor, doctor, I can't stop the thought I might be dying of syphilis.

—I don't think you are, said Dr Burns, but with an air of resignation.

—But I could be.

—Very well, the doctor said. I'll make a referral for you to the Special Clinic, where you'll be seen by a specialist. But I think it's a waste of time. I don't think they'll find anything.

—Thank you, thank you, doctor! How long will it take?

—You'll be sent a letter. They are busy places, but they usually see you within two to three weeks.

One day two weeks later he came home from school. His mum had a worried look.

—There's a letter came for you today with a hospital frank on it. I was so worried I opened it. You're

wanted at an appointment for a 'Special Clinic'.
What's that all about?

—I don't know, he said. He thought, with accuracy or not, that often his mother didn't understand the world, so he said, —Maybe that's just something they send out to different people every year. Like a kind of survey or a general check up. I'll go next Wednesday and see.

It was the day before his Biology exam. He should have been studying for it. It was tremendously wet, the whole day. A huge depression came in over the Firth of Clyde and dumped inches of rain across Ayrshire in twelve hours. It started when he was standing at the bottom of the lane waiting for the bus to Ayr on the morning that, he thought, was to decide his future.

The appointment was at Heathfield hospital on the outskirts of Ayr. Jed sat in the bus near the back with its windows steamed up by all the passengers' breaths and rubbed a porthole in the cool, misty pane where trickles of rain seeped lachrymosely down the glass like the sporadic movements of tadpoles over pond mud in shallow water. The bus drove up the coast for part of its route. Somewhere out there, in their other world, the gannets would be spearing into the Clyde or wheeling, low, through the rainmist with the black triangles of their wingtips contrasting with the slim blades of the white wings and looking as if their tips had been dipped, with precision, in a pot of black paint. He had found one dead along the shore of Irvine beach recently when he was taking part in a sponsored school walk—a huge bird in a tangle of soiled feather, half-buried in sand, the faint mustard glow of the white forehead and the faded blue of the bladed beak below a round, still-open eye. Sometimes, he learned, they broke their necks by misjudging and diving into too-shallow water.

The bus was hot and humid with soaked coats and bodies. It jolted over every bump in the road. It took fifty minutes to reach the outskirts of Ayr. He got off at the stop the bus driver said and asked directions to the hospital from an impatient man sheltering half-hidden under a wide umbrella. Rain was drumming steadily along the pavements and running in floods along the gutters at roof edges and down the syvers. A purging. The walk, among suburban buildings, took him twenty minutes. He had no umbrella— it wasn't really a concept he recognised—and the whole sky emptied its weight onto the coast.

By the time he reached the hospital reception he was not only soaked through but his clothes weighed twice what they would normally and clung to him uncomfortably. He went to the back of the queue at the receptionist's window, slopping with Atlantic water that dripped from him and made a puddle around his feet where he stood.

—Next.

He stepped forward.

—Some details please. Name?

He gave it.

—Address?

He gave it.

—Next of kin?

This was unexpected. His mother? His father? And did it mean they would be *contacted?* Also it raised the thought that he either might not get out of the hospital alive or that he was dying.

—Next of kin?

He gave his father's name.

—Follow the arrows down that corridor and turn left. Wait in the first waiting area on the right.

He walked squelching and slowly down the corridor, like a man wearing a wet suit of armour. In the waiting area, two nurses were talking in quiet voices to a man sitting impassively.

—Your wife will have to come in and see us too, one said.

—Does that have tae happen? said the man.

—Yes, said the nurse. —She might have been infected.

Wide ramifying networks of infection and disease in forgotten circumstances grew their dark branches backward through his brain cells, like some sort of horrible fungi.

The nurses went away, leaving him and the man who sat head-bowed and oblivious to him.

A nurse reappeared. —Dr Schofield will see you now, she said.

Dr Schofield was a tall German-sounding man with hair as white as the breast of a herring gull. He was smoking a thick cigar when Jed walked in, and stubbed it out in a cloud of blue in the ashtray before him on the desk.

—Sit, he said, and scrutinised in silence for some few minutes the notes in the file before him.

Jed sat and watched him.

—So, the doctor said finally, looking up, you think you have syphilis eh? Tell me why you think that.

He repeated his story. There was no hint of ridicule or disbelief with this doctor however. He listened carefully. When he had finished, the doctor said:

—It doesn't seem very likely that you have this disease from this account. First of all, a chancre tends to be a very nasty looking sore, not the spot you describe. But to make sure we will give you a blood test. Now, this is a 100% accurate diagnostic test for the presence of syphilis. Do you understand what that means? If it's negative, you don't have anything wrong with you. After all, and here he smiled, we wouldn't want you infecting half the young women in Ayrshire. But we should examine you too, though it is unlikely to reveal anything to us at this point. Step over there please, and drop your pants.

He did as he was asked. The doctor took his member, shrunken and concertina'd up at the foreskin by the cold and the wet of Atlantic weather, and matter of factly pushed back the foreskin all around it, examined it, and probed his testicles, which sagged chastenedly in their wrinkled bag.

—Thank you. You may dress again. Sit please.

He sat back down. The doctor looked at him across the table. —There is nothing there to discover, he said. —In a few minutes I will call the nurse and she will take a blood sample for a test—and remember, this is 100% accurate. It either confirms the presence of the disease or it does not. If it does, we treat it with penicillin. But in this case I don't think it will. Now, do you understand all that?

—Yes, doctor. Thank you, doctor.

—No, thank *you*. You are a very responsible young man. Phone me one week today for the result of the test, between noon and 1pm. Here is the number. The doctor wrote it down on a slip of paper. —I'll now fetch the nurse, who will take your blood.

He had never had blood taken before so he did not know not to look as the tourniquet was wrapped round his arm below his rolled-up sleeve, and the thin needle was plunged deep into the bulged vein where it ran, muscly and thick, over the inside of his right elbow and the little tube filled with the dark rich red. That was him. That was his life.

When he emerged from the hospital, the rain had stopped. Bits of gleam were appearing in the unrelenting grey above the town. His clothes were only sodden now, not slopped-wet-through, partly dried by his body heat.

—What happened at the hospital? his mother said when he got back.

—Oh, a lot of nonsense. I don't even know why I was asked to go.

No more was said on the matter.

★

How did he get through the week of agonised waiting? He had no memory how, unless minute by minute. He had an exam on the morning of the day he was due to phone. It finished at noon. There was a phone box at Irvine Cross. He made sure he had enough change for half an hour of peak-rate phone calls. He rang the number at five minutes past twelve and, when it was answered and the blips started, shoved the 50p into the slot. The blips stopped and he was connected.

—Reception, Heathfield Hospital.

—Can I speak to Dr Schofield please?

—One moment.

Another voice came on which he recognised as the doctor.

—Dr Schofield?

—Ah yes. The young man who saw me last week. What was your name again?

He gave it.

—I am happy to say your results were entirely satisfactory.

This was too ambiguous for someone who needed absolute clarity. As if sensing this, the doctor added, —That is, your blood test was clear. Remember, this is a 100% accurate test. *There is nothing wrong with you.*

—Oh thank you, doctor!

—No, thank *you*. And now, enjoy your life.

It was a sunlit day in May, and the afternoon was clear of exams. A bunch of boys were going to play football on a patch of green above the riverbank near the school. He joined in, a boy having been given his life back, springing around till he was pouring with sweat, pure body under the incandescent sun.

★

Thereafter, by degrees, the threat that he was dying from that particular disease receded, fading into the distance like a dark and jungled island sailed away from, though he would be disturbed occasionally by sudden irrational thoughts. He was given a lift once by Graham Moses, a near-neighbour on the caravan site, who worked repairing medical machines. Stopping at a garage, he was rummaging under the back seat for something, muttering, 'They should be here somewhere, among these specimens of bad blood'— a rack of little test tubes.

The thought suddenly came to him: *what if his test tube had been mixed up by mistake with someone else's?* The thought would leap the demon of his fear into brief life, but even for him this scenario seemed an unlikelihood, and it soon slept again.

What was it all about, at root? It was a desire for purity. Around this time he found himself being viscerally disgusted by ugliness. It was an extension of an emotion he had sometimes felt looking at particular photographs in some of his nature books. There was one of a small variety of puffer fish in an encyclopaedia of wildlife, which Charles the Prince of Wales—signing himself, regally, in his own handwriting, 'Charles'—had written a foreword for; a little fish whose body appeared to consist of hexagonal cells. This held a strange fascination for Jed, a variety of disgust that was not so extreme that it stopped him revisiting the photograph to experience the emotion anew. There was another photograph of a caribou back, flayed of its hide, that had been parasitised by warble flies, which

lay eggs in the fur; the grubs burrowed below
the skin and pupated there. This hide was pocked
with the blood-edged holes those grubs had made
in the caribou's back, was riddled with them; exit
holes. This too held a strange fascination. It would
be only many years later he would come across a
name for this, Trypophobia. This revulsion could be
prompted, more strongly, by other things such as a
splatter of trodden-on chips on the dark tarmac of
a pavement in the rain, or a mass of discarded ash
and cigarette butts that someone had tipped from a
car ashtray onto the kerb. Such sights would almost
burn themselves into his retina like the after-image
of the sun looked at too directly, and then print
themselves into his brain where they could only be
removed if he imagined them being incinerated in
a roar of flame every time they intruded into his
unblemished mind. Once, he had smudged with
mucky fingers a page of his treasured *AA Book of
British Birds*, the page about binoculars which showed
a flying tern under two strengths of magnification.
This smudge of muck on the glossy white page of
something that was important to him so unsettled
him that he had to 'correct' it by occluding the
worst of the stain with a blue fibretip pen, leaving a
peculiar irregularly shaped blotch that looked much
worse than the original smudge. This horror of
imperfection did not extend to other things out in
nature: he had no problem for instance in handling
bird skulls which were among the objects he
collected after his egg-collecting days were finished.
He had read about the pectinated claw by which

PLATE 22

THE LESSER TERN

herons comb off eel slime by mixing it with special powder-making feathers on their breast. When he found—the excitement!—a dead heron in a marsh, he went straight to one of the big, grey, antidiluvian feet, reptilian and a perfect proof that birds are descended from dinosaurs, found the claw with its little notches along the outer edge of the keratin— the precision of it, the detail!—and cut the foot off with a little penknife, sawing vigorously through the bone, sinew and tendon of the cold grey faintly malodorous scaliness, and finally snapping it like a twig. He carried the foot home in his coat pocket, intending to keep it till he could work out how to get the claw itself. After a while, he managed to just slip it off like a little sheath. He experienced no such flashback horrors at the sight of a decaying heron.

Around this time, along with skull and owl pellets, he also began collecting feathers, any that interested him as he wandered the landscape. Under the bed in his bedroom the shoeboxes accumulated, containing the fur of rodents dissected from owl pellets, and the little skulls and jawbones were arranged with the bigger bird skulls on top of his small chest of drawers. He would sellotape carefully the particularly interesting feathers into his big notebook along with some notes about what type of feather it was—where on the bird's body it had come from— and where he'd found it. He identified these from the detailed paintings of individual species by Raymond Harris Ching in the AA book. As part of this he discovered that when birds moult their feathers as happens every year they do so in a symmetrical pattern, which is especially important in the wings; this is so the wings keep their aerodynamic effectiveness and are not made lopsided by asymmetric absences. He also discovered new words: 'barbules', the tiny filament-hooks—from the Latin *barbula*, 'a little beard'—that interlock on a bird's feather and form, from its many barbs, one flat aerodynamic surface; 'vermiculations': the fine barring on, say, a duck's breast feather, with its slightly fluffy base and its inbuilt curvature echoing the breast's roundness. Among his prizes were a nightjar's feather found at a Hampshire heath edge on a summer holiday and a sparrowhawk primary feather, given glamour in the old sense of 'glamourie', a magical spell, by the fact that it had circled, in the bird's wing perhaps, high above the county diminished to a rotating map below as the bird soared, as sparrowhawks at times are prone to do. It was a piece of wildness in his caravan bedroom. For a while he even sent away for feathers he could not find in the Ayrshire landscape around him, discovered from a supplier in an advert in the *Exchange & Mart*. These were intended for fly-tying by fishermen, but could serve a feather-collecting schoolboy just as well. So he came to possess golden pheasant feathers, and the small, azure and black-barred feather from the wing of a jay, resplendent and detailed and perfect.

★

It was O-grade season. He never understood why, as with Good Friday, unless for maximum punishment, the exam season came round just as the world was waking to the ecstasy of spring, birds nesting everywhere, the new light opening the beeches all across Ayrshire. Hundreds of teenagers at Irvine Royal were powered by the same forces that had the peewits tumbling and whooping and throat-huskily crying over the fresh-seeded barley fields up country—locked down to days studying arithmetic, French, chemistry, geography, to guarantee a future. How did everyone stand it? He would be out in the light evenings walking the Annick Water upriver and hearing the first common sandpipers, just back from Africa—*Africa!*—on the river bank. It was astonishment, under the sun.

PLATE 13.

JAY.

Stewart del.

They would file into Mrs Murray's English class in the too-hot classroom on brilliant afternoons. Some higher authority had decided that Ted Hughes' 'The Jaguar' was what they should be studying that year.

'The apes yawn and adore their fleas in the sun.'

—Why adore? the teacher asked.

—Because they're bored, Miss.

—Good, good. Why is the boa-constrictor's coil like 'a fossil'?

—Miss, what's a boa-constrictor?

—A kind of snake, Gillian.

Thirty youngsters were rampant with hormones on a gorgeous spring afternoon while eggs were cracking open with new life all over the county and a cock blackbird, gold beak coiled with faintly writhing pink, swooped up onto the stone wall outside the windows and poised there for a moment, flaring out its tail feathers in a fan and closing them again. The class tried to get its collective head into the soporific afternoon scene of the heatwaved zoo. The poem's 'bang of blood' left Jed quite untouched. What did that mean? He had never had much time for zoos. He had not seen one since he was a little boy. 'Over the cage floor the horizons come.' The teacher explained that this was the fantasy of the jaguar. Jed could not summon up much interest in jaguars either. You didn't see any in the fields around Ayrshire.

He would look idly through the book they used at the back of the class and there, to his considerable surprise, he discovered something. There was a poem-extract called 'Reynard's Last Run'. 'The earth was stopped. It was barred with stakes.' It was written in tumpity-tump rhyme and was about a fox being chased by a hunt. The sound of the poem was the running of the fox—over the downs, up the slopes, down the other sides, across the entire landscape pursued by baying hounds. He could see the same hounds out with the Annick Hunt on many Saturday mornings. The riders in their resplendent red jackets, breeches white as milk, and boot-black caps, spurring the swollen veiny sides of the great horses and galloping after the pack of beagles, dark brown and white and chestnut, with their stiffly up-curved tails wagging, all to the brassy sound of the huntsman's horn.

To his own surprise, while everyone sweated and furrowed their brows over Ted Hughes' yawn-inducing jaguar for which the teacher explained the reason for every word, he would sit head-down surreptitiously at the back of the class and read the fox poem for pleasure. He was away with that fox, at speed, pursued. And there was something about the man who had written it. He was on the side of the fox, not of the hounds or the red coats galloping through the woods and jumping over the hedges. Jed was the fox in the class, and the teacher, and the exams and educational system, that wanted them all to be safe in their studying of Ted Hughes' jaguar, were the zoo. It was the first time he experienced something in a poem not force-fed to him by a teacher. It was his; he owned it. It was like the tawny owl in the witchwood across the river: a secret.

★

When the exam season was over—all those mornings and afternoons of silent invigilation at your isolated desks, like little square islands in a regimented archipelago, the invigilator pacing around silently, hands clasped behind his back, like a heron, then the bell and the onrush of light and chatter outside, and the huge sky beyond the invigilation hall— something strange happened. He discovered that he didn't need to go to school. It was the end of fourth year. Some pupils were leaving. Some, like him, were going into fifth year. In the weeks till the end of term there was a relaxed air in the school; if you didn't turn up to lessons no one seemed to notice, or if they did, to mind.

The beech leaves were thickening and darkening. Most of the birds no longer had eggs but were feeding chicks and fledgelings scattered around the hedges and thickets and woods. Cats pounced on the succulent plumpness of young blackbirds. The world of Wimbledon with its immaculate tennis whites, its commentators' 'I *say*!' at a particularly impressive point-scoring forehand drive, its tennis superstars in their world of perfection reduced to a tennis court, a world of reasonableness, hinted-at luxury and affluence and mannerliness, and their athletes' cleanliness and fitness, beguiled him by its contrast to the everyday reality in which he lived. He did not know where he was going. He did not know what would happen. He did not even think about such things. The daily intensity of the birds' singing would start to fade like an afterglow. The whole landscape sank into a midsummer haze where the vegetation rose outrageously in the hedge bottoms and the woods were heavy and green. It was heading towards, for him, one of the least interesting times of the year for birds, till he discovered the autumn migrations that began in late summer.

The other boy on the site had told him that sometimes Davy Smith at Middleton needed help with singling neeps so one day, as he walked past the farmyard with him, they turned right, on impulse, and entered the square in front of the big house surrounded by outbuildings. It was a hot May day after the last exam. The light fell on the farmyard in full heat, and in the silence a swallow swooped into an outbuilding to be met by the sudden applause of twitters as it fed the young, before darting out again, a small dark flickerer, against a white cloud silently exploding up in the blue.

They knocked on the door in the silence. There was no answer, so they knocked again. There was the sound of stirring inside the house.

—Ah'll handle this, the other boy said. An old lady scraped the door open and looked at them suspiciously.

—Hey missus, any work for us?

—Where you fae? the old woman said.

—The caravan site. Baith o us.

—Ye ken the deefrence atween charlock an neeps?

—Aye.

—Ye singled neeps afore?

—Aye.

—Come back the morn. Nine o'clock. Davy'll likely stert ye.

—Thanks missus.

Out on the main road again, walking back to the caravan site driveway, the other boy said, —See? Keep it short an simple.

The following morning they were back in the relative freshness of 8.30am. He felt exposed and vulnerable in the face of the new. Davy Smith the farmer wore hobnail boots and dark baggy trousers hoisted and held to mid-stomach by braces over a shirt the colour of dark mustard. He had huge, ham-like forearms, the upper sides of which were scaly with ringworm which he would scratch incessantly, loosening the flakes of white in little blizzards with fingernails dark-crescented with earth.

—Ye singled neeps afore? he said.

—Yes. (He hadn't.)

—Gid. Come oot tae the field wi me on the back o the trailer.

The hard boards of the trailer on the back of the tractor under your buttock bones, the wince when it jerked going over a pothole, the deafening gutturals and spitting of the tractor engine and vertical exhaust. They turned out of the farm, swaying and creaking, went left down the lane, accelerated unexpectedly in the blue morning so he was almost pitched onto his back, and turned right into the field; he gripped the edge of the trailer tightly, being swayed from side to side in its motion. Then the engine off. The ticking silence as it cooled. They stood at the top of a field bounded on two sides by hedges, filled with neat rows—'dreels', as he soon learned they were called—of green seedlings in little clusters and groups stretching all down the dreels.

Davy Smith handed him, bafflingly, two sacks and some bailer twine.

—Wrap they roon yer knees, he said. He showed him how, then demonstrated singling neeps—weeding out all but a single seedling every six inches or so, to give it room to grow, with the muscly fingers of a lifetime of manual labour.

—Lik that, see? he said. —Or ye can dae it wi the hoe.

—He stood upright, took the hoe, and separated a single seedling from a little clump of them with the hoe's small lateral blade. This was a much fussier operation; it was easier on hands and knees with your fingers and thumbs.

Jed stood and looked across the rows and rows of green. They had the whole field to do!

The days now took on a particular pattern. They would work in relative silence through the morning, moving up and down the dreels methodically, brushing away from either side of the chosen seedling along its raised row of earth the little clusters of others and leaving them in valleys between the dreels to wither whitely in the sun. The soil was dry and crumbling in the hot weather; your hands developed calluses. He was conscientious even with something as ultimately meaningless, some may have thought, as this and he worked hard, up and down, soon pouring dark sweat onto the crumbly pale soil, standing up occasionally to stretch his back and survey the field. The morning sessions, he discovered, were the hardest. There was no break between nine and twelve. Then, at noon, Davy Smith would trudge unannounced back towards the tractor and trailer and the field edge and he and whoever else had joined them on that day would know this was a signal to follow suit. No one ever missed the signal. They leapt onto the back of the trailer, and back it would go to the farm; the tractor engine's spitting roar, and a bit of breeze fanning your forehead as it rushed along the lane, were both welcome after the morning's silence and stillness. The landscape sped by: soon the whole swaying, creaking contraption had turned into the farmyard and you were standing again in ticking silence after launching yourself off the hard boards.

Lunch was a high point of the day. You would be ushered into the cool dim kitchen out of the glare and dazzle of the farmyard and take your seat at the round table. The food was plain—boiled potatoes, meat, and vegetables, and a pudding of custard, say, and jam roll, or some other variation, followed by a mug of tea. Occasionally a car would pass on the road outside on the way to Irvine or in the opposite direction to Stewarton. Otherwise there would be mainly silence, punctuated by the slow tick of an old wall-clock. The farmhouse was huge. He thought of all the rooms laid out above and beyond where they sat. Davy Smith was unmarried. He shared this space with his two sisters. The one who served the food was, Jed thought, kindly. She had answered the door when he and the other boy had first asked about work. The other was white-haired with her expression settled into a rictus of pain, ill-temper and dissatisfaction. If he had been an insightful boy he would have wondered what their life was like here in this big house and what had happened to them to bring them to this, but instead he merely watched the housefly's glee as it rubbed its front legs together on the solid brick of butter, one end irregular from the men's scrapings, and noticed the weight of the old woman's calves, shapeless as the legs of elephants, sagging over her plain brown shoes in her thick brown stockings.

After food Davy Smith would lie on a little bench against the wall on his back with a copy of *The Glasgow Herald* unfolded like wings over his face, rising and falling with his breaths. At exactly 1pm he would grab the newspaper in a scrunched-up gathering in one hand, sit up, muttering, and swing his legs round onto the floor. The work for the afternoon was about to begin.

The afternoon was easier because, at around 3.30pm, Davy Smith's sister would materialise through the heat-shimmer rising from the field, enlarging as she approached, with a basket over one arm carrying sandwiches, biscuits, tea and diluted orange juice, which she left in the shade of a hedge.

Whoever was working in the field that afternoon would walk up and sit below the hedge and be served by Davy. The last ninety minutes or so till 5pm were easy. You had just had food and rest in the shade of the hedge. Jed had not yet been introduced to the concept of the visual beauty of the white clouds moving across the blue and the shadows of swallows weaving across the lit ground before the sitting men, but it was there. You were buoyed by the idea of stopping soon. Then it was the rattling creaking journey back again to the farmyard. Then with an air of ceremony Davy would pull his wallet from his pocket and extract two single pound notes—your wages for the day.

—Ye'll be back the morn?

PLATE 27.

CHIMNEY SWALLOW.

—Yes.

—Gid.

Jed would walk the short distance up the lane to the caravan site, aching in every limb.

This went on for several days until, one afternoon of fierce sun, he took his shirt off as he moved up the rows on his hands and knees and let the heat and the light pour down, full, from the unclouded blue for three hours, square onto his adolescent-broadening shoulders. It was only when he got home at the end of that day that he realised he had overdone it. His back, when he stripped off his shirt and looked at it in the mirror was a violent pinkish-red, a dermatological exclamation mark. He could feel the stored solar energy it had absorbed boiling and agitating inside it.

—What were you doing taking yer shirt off? his mother said, exasperated.

—It was roasting in the field, mum. I didn't think I had my shirt off very long.

That night, he could not lie on his back. By the following morning big water blisters had erupted all across his shoulder blades and across the tops of his shoulders.

At 10.30am there was a knock at the door of the caravan. He could hear Davy Smith from his bedroom, where he lay on his stomach with his back radiating heat enough to fry eggs on.

—Jed in, missus?

He came out of his bedroom to the door, where Davy was standing below the step. Jed was baretorsoed as he could not bear a shirt against his skin.

—I can't come today, Davy. I've burnt myself.

After three or four days when the blisters had all burst and dribbled away in water, his back began peeling and itching; long strips of skin like wallpaper developed that he could pull from the tops of his shoulders with a strange pleasure, a primate making itself clean. He did not work at the neeps any more that summer. Like Jed, a range of people had dropped in for a day or two or longer and then drifted off again.

These had included Tam Lusk, a local man with a physique like a champion boxer's, who could speed up and down the dreels with an Achilles-like ease and facility, much as he complained about the backbreaking nature of the work. He smoked roll-ups; the scent of nicotine in the still afternoons of early summer in the field. Often the labourers would dislodge from the dreels white clay smoking pipes, 'cutties' of men who had worked in these same fields generations ago and were now nameless dust. Jed would watch the dance of the muscles, their continual alterations, in Tam Lusk's arms as he moved up the dreels; the bulge of the bicep with a vein in it as Tam put a cupped match to the roll-up between his lips. Jed respected him because of his physique but also his manner which was less that of the easy-oasy joking of, say, Davy Smith, as if too many difficult things had happened to Tam Lusk for him to consider everything a joke, and more a general sense that all was difficult and would be difficult. Lusk's attitude towards Davy Smith was one of grudging but not obeisant acceptance that

Davy owned the land and had the money. At the end of the day he would be paid four pounds in single green notes, twice that of the teenage boys' wages.

Jed saw him a little later that summer, in heatwave weather, down the lane of the caravan site. It had been a hot season. Tam was wearing a bush hat, under which he smiled broadly, his deeply tanned and seamed face and neck brown as a conker. He was a completely different person from the man who had singled neeps for Davy Smith. The happiness radiated from him like light from the sun.

—Is this no the life, eh? We could dae wi weeks mair o this.

Tam Lusk had been picking brambles from the embankment of the railway line, casting them into a small bucket full of the black fruit, each a little cluster of smaller segments like the eyes of large insects, traversed here and there by a small pale grub raising the front part of its body as if scanning a far horizon.

Several weeks later, on a grey autumn morning, Davy Smith flagged Jed down at the verge as he cycled past Middleton.

—Ye hear the news aboot Tam Lusk? he said.

—No.

—Deid. Workin in a field and jist drapped deid. He wis awa in meenits.

Jed's first reaction was astonishment that a man with such a physique could die. He thought muscles were a protection against the universe. But he also noticed that Davy Smith seemed strangely excited to be telling him this news as if the dead man was a sacrificial victim who had been taken instead of him, Davy.

—Ye'd no a thocht it, eh? he said. —Anely a young man tae. An he looked sae fit.

He did not work for Davy Smith again with the exception of a single morning that October when he had asked him if there were any jobs.

—Shawin neeps, said Davy. He took him out in the tractor to the field they'd singled the neeps in during the summer. It was a grey morning, with a threat of rain.

—This is whit ye dae, he said, lifting the turnips by their green leafy tops and, with a single stroke, severing the green stalks from the big irregular sphere of the vegetable, which you simply let drop back in the field, and cast the handful of green stalks aside.

—Come back tae the hoose at twelve, said Davy.

He left Jed there, alone in the field, and as he worked in the Saturday morning silence it began to rain and grew heavier and heavier. He worked for an hour until the field was a plastered quagmire of glutinous glaur that sucked at his wellington boots with each step he took among a chaos of strewn stalks and shawed neeps with the flesh still creamy-fresh where it had been cut. His hair was flattened wet onto his forehead and soon his clothes clung to him as if they'd been thickly pasted on.

He lasted till lunchtime when he trudged, slipping and sliding, back through the sucking mud to the farmhouse.

—I'm stopping, he told Davy.

—Aye. Too dreich for ye, eh.

—Yes.

He was paid a single pound note. Many years later he would read an episode in *Tess of the D'Urbervilles* in which Tess has exactly the same experience, but for the whole day.

★

It was August suddenly and the schools went back in the middle of the month, like a reminder that August weather was not something to be enjoyed and lost in, but a distraction merely from the real things of life, its rules and discipline. The world was moving towards fruiting and seed and harvest. All the birds had stopped singing. The swifts had gone, back to Africa, their scythe wings flicking through the blue. The swallows would soon begin congregating, twitteringly, on telegraph wires like young men excited by the outbreak of war.

He suspected that something was afoot when he went back to Irvine Royal and in the English class the teacher came over to his desk and asked 'Are you Gerard Cambridge?'

—Yes, he said, immediately alarmed to be singled out and identified.

—Well done. Your exam results for the O Grade were the first in the year for English in the whole school.

He felt immediately split between a vague small pleasure at having 'won' something and incredulity at how it had come about. How could it have happened? He had only written about nature. In one sense he had hijacked the exam, interpreting its questions brazenly in favour of his own predilections.

Apart from the small pleasure at this distinction he found that it was almost entirely to his disadvantage.

He had felt that if you really wanted something you should always imagine it was not going to happen which, by some sort of inverse magic, meant that it might. He had an instinctive revulsion in his tawny-owl-like secrecy against being spotlit by an expectation that something he might do would be good. Now, though, the English teachers appeared to have such expectations of him. He was no longer anonymous. He was that boy who had come first in the year for the O-grade exam. They began asking him difficult questions about, say, societal tension in the relationship between Romeo and Juliet, or Winston Smith's attitude toward authority and whether it was justified. His redfaced tonguetied silence was evidence that his exam result was a fluke and this of course increased his embarrassment. He was shown to be a fraud for a distinction which he had never claimed for himself in the first place. After a month or so of such awkward spotlighting, the teachers gave him up in a tacit acknowledgement that they had been mistaken in their expectations. He was able to sink back into a more comfortable, camouflaged obscurity where nothing insightful or remarkable was expected from him. He had always had an instinctive belief in being underestimated. That way you might surprise people with unanticipated achievement, and if you didn't then no disappointment on their part was involved. He could also sense again that an expressed high expectation on the part of another could come from a covert malevolence and a desire to see you fail, masquerading as high opinion. If no one assumed anything of anyone, it cleared a free space in which something interesting might happen. It made failure no great deal, and therefore the striving for something spectacular or original possible.

★

That winter, the year of studying for Highers, there was an AA bus company strike between October and December for eight weeks. This was a legitimate reason for him not to go to school: he couldn't get there. He felt an uneasy, ambiguous combination of freedom, worry that some punishment might be meted out to him by the authorities, and a sense that he was missing out on important things that might be happening among his friends. Of course, he could have got to school if he had really wanted to. He could have walked the four miles each way, an hour's trek, and not much to him. But society's expectation for what was acceptable and his own were, at that point, far apart. How far was too far? How much was too much? So he didn't go to school, enjoying the delicious sense of liberation from timetables. Instead he had to make his own routine. A big part of this consisted in walking down to the floodpool at Warwickdale on the way to Springside, a pool that developed in two fields forming a bowl surrounded by hills. There were little bankings dotted with hawthorns that you could approach the pool under cover behind, and crawl up on your hands and knees, and lie at full length on, peeking over at whatever might be there. It was a magnet for passing birds, an oasis, a bare eye of water gazing at the open sky and gathering wading birds, ducks and swans like light into it.

He had a set routine for visiting this, usually between 11am and 1pm, and would be away down the lane with his loping strides, and across three fields, including the bottom edge of the field he'd singled neeps in that summer. His routine slowed to the routine of birds, the routine of landscape, mornings of frost, when the hard gray glitter lay across everything, having been open to the Universe all night: intimations of interstellar cold, his breath puffing out in clouds of body warmth into the silent morning and his cheeks stinging with adolescent blood.

He had many good sightings at this floodpool. He never knew what might turn up. It gave his late mornings a sense of anticipation. His approach to the main pool was 'blind', obscured by thickets and bankings, so often he did not know what was there till the last moment when his head inched over the top, cautiously, like a man nervy for sniper fire, then he swept across the water's surface and all the margins with the bright, dark-surrounded circle of magnifying light, soundless and secretly intrusive. Once it was Whooper swans, birds of light with their yellow and black bills and their uneasy belling notes repeated concernedly among each other in the tall throats like bells in church steeples, heads-up alerted, drifting leftwards in a breeze riffling the water's surface as it riffled up their feather tips along their backs. Exotic, on their way from Iceland, yet here they were, dropping in so the boy unable to get to school because of a bus strike could see them on a November morning entirely placeless and timeless to them. Sometimes he would hear their faintly metallic belling overhead from the schoolgrounds of Irvine Royal and feel pride and privilege that these sounds meant so much to him and so little— nothing—to most of his schoolfriends, even had they known what they were. But they didn't. The sounds were his alone, a secret like the secret of his being a Catholic, but unlike that not hedged about by danger of violent discovery.

The Whoopers, a group of fifteen or so, stayed for several days. He got used to seeing them, their wariness showing that they were truly wild and thus a greater gift to him. Then, one morning, the pond was simply empty of the fifteen white presences. He felt strangely bereft. They had flown, observing realities that had nothing to do with boys or school lessons or shops or the history of the Catholic church and Protestantism in Irvine.

He had become, almost without realising it, very strange about food. It had begun after his failed attempts to transmogrify into Hercules II. He had cut out lunch at school, mainly, so his body had grown used to the long fast between 8am and almost 5pm. Now, without the discipline of the school days, he had to find a new pattern and he did this by slipping slowly into a punitive abstinence that made him feel virtuous and, even, holy. He became locked in a pattern of resistance to food and assailed and harangued by his mother. 'Get that down you will you, an stop bein so fussy!' This new approach of his was an advantage when you had a father who

1 The Hooper. 2 The Mute Swan. 3 The Polish Swan. 4 Bewick's Swan.

PLATE 2*

did not like the amount of food you ate. His father's threatening, hovering presence simply buttressed what he was doing anyway now, which was to eat less. It turned his father's grudge into an ally. He felt lightheaded at times, but he was thrilled by the effect his new routine had on his body. It was a form of magic, of shapeshifting. Late at night he would examine himself in the mirror, seeing how, in the electric lighting, his ribs were starting to show in their bony cage and the cords in his neck when he turned his head had a strange, newly visible beauty. The great shape of his pelvic girdle began to appear and reveal itself, jutting at his hips. The little white-haired cadaverous priest's holding aloft of the Communion host between his two thumbs and forefingers took on a holiness he shared. He could subsist on crumbs too if it came to it.

Food was a central feature of the family dynamic. His mother was constantly trying to foist on him— as he saw it—fried breakfasts, fat-rich foods lardy with cholesterol, while Gayelord Hauser, nutritional expert to rich Americans, advocated brown rice, black molasses, fruit and vegetables. His father was top animal and had to have the best food, such as sirloin steak on a Saturday night. This was a sun around which all the planets of lesser needs, his own, his mother's and sisters', orbited. He had begun close to the sun. Now he was becoming like Pluto, cold and remote, beyond caring. The emotional investment in such a thing as a piece of meat seemed to him laughable.

One morning of frost he lay bonily shivering

and gazing through his Zenoptems at a bunch of redshanks at the edge of the floodpool at Warwickdale: some preening their back feathers; some standing on one leg with their bills tucked into their backs; some picking their way carefully along the water margins on their orange-red stilts, pecking carefully at something invisible in front of them with the long beaks. He noticed a different bird among their ordinariness. It looked similar, but its legs were yellow. At first he thought this a strange variety of redshank, an aberration of the same species. But he found it using the keys for identification in Roger Tory Peterson's *A Field Guide to the Birds of Britain and Europe*, part of his expanding library of bird books. A Lesser Yellowlegs. He was still naive enough to think that a rare bird would come with some sort of announcement of its rarity, as if a millionaire would come with a placard. From the call box on the caravan site, that night, his breath misting the pane, the receiver cold against his ear, he phoned W. R.—Bill—Brackenridge, the secretary for the Scottish Ornithologist's Club, who lived in Ayr. He was in his mid-twenties and had once or twice taken Jed out looking for nightjars around Montgreenan. Bill Brackenridge was a small, neat, compact man who for him represented a great sanity and civility in the world of birds, compared with his life at home and in school.

—Bill, I think I've found a rare bird.

—Which one?

—A Lesser Yellowlegs.

There was a dubious pause. —Are you sure?

PLATE 15

COMMON TOTANUS

SPOTTED TOTANUS

—No. That's why I'm telling you.

—Why do you think it's that?

—It has yellow legs. And it looks a bit different from the redshanks it's with.

—Where is it?

—At the floodpool at Warwickdale on the Overtoun Road, near Springside.

—I'll get there tomorrow morning at ten. Can you meet me there?

—Yes.

—See you then.

The next day was a Saturday. He could see Bill Brackenridge's car at the edge of the road beside the pool, the single cylinder of a telescope resting against the top edge of the rolled-down window. Jed approached by his usual route, and scanned the floodpool margin. The bird was still there.

Bill Brackenridge saw him from his own vantage. Not long afterwards he drove away up the Overtoun Road and parked in the verge out of sight and beyond disturbance of the feeding redshanks and their far-travelled associate. Jed backtracked, swung round across a top field, and walked down the road to meet him.

Bill came out of the car and stood leaning against the bonnet.

—Well?

—It is. Who'd ever have thought it. A Lesser Yellowlegs.

—I thought it was. I'm glad you were able to check.

—You'll be able to get a job as a tour guide soon, Bill Brackenridge quipped. Busloads of ornithologists will be turning up to see this if it sticks around. Anyway, well done. And well spotted and identified.

—I wonder how it got here from America?

—Blown off course. That's how a lot of these vagrants end up on this side of the Atlantic.

Bill Brackenridge's response to this rare sighting was part of Jed's growing awareness of the live network of birdwatchers, ringers and tickers who formed part of a whole alternative subculture of a civilised world far beyond home and school, what seemed a world of order and reasonableness. He did not aspire to it and did not think he could be a part of it. It involved cars and telescopes and therefore money, which he did not have. His aspirations were, otherwise, completely bourgeois. Sometimes, walking a little past Irvine Cross if he decided to get the bus for home—when it was not on strike—he would pass in the winter twilight the affluent, detached houses of the douce middle-class—little cells of lamplight with bookcases and tables, and never a person to be seen. That was what he aspired to. Privilege was space. He did not feel himself privileged despite the miles of landscape all around him on the caravan site.

More and more he presented a gaunt aspect to the world, but it was never enough. He always felt too heavy. But he was in full control of what came into his body by mouth. His lightheadedness continued and he noticed that one of his curses for the years of his adolescence, his blushes, stopped. His face in fact would barely flush at all. His body did not have the necessary fuel to generate the additional heat that was the throbbing open heart of his sinfulness made visible.

Just before Christmas the bus strike ended, but it was too close to the school holidays for him to feel pressured into going back to school for a few days. So his return was left until the new year. A school friend had passed on details of what he should be studying in the different lessons, but he had not missed much. The chemistry teacher in his class of seven or eight brave souls doing Higher Chemistry would enter at the beginning of the lesson, hands clasped behind his back. He was a small man in a sombre jacket who reeked of cigarettes when he paced past you as you sat head bowed to some inexplicable passage in your textbook. The teacher's face was set into deep grooves and lines. He would have been handsome once. Now he was small, bowed and wizened by nicotine. His teaching style was this:

—Open your textbooks to chapter thirteen and read it, please.

He would then pace pensively, gazing in silence before him, hands still clasped together behind his back, around the ancient, dim classroom with its long wooden benches arranged like seats in chapel. Each time he reached the rear of the class which adjoined a little staffroom, he would disappear for some minutes. At intervals he would reappear, and ask into the silence:

—Any questions?

Few of the pupils, and certainly not Jed, ever had any questions. They were nervy of the consequences and endless tedium that might result if they asked this man a question about chemistry.

★

He was worried about the strangeness he would feel on returning to school after such an extended break, especially when there had been nothing wrong with him! It was only a bus strike. His eating now had a strict routine, often two slices of thin white toast at breakfast, smeared with the faintest sleeking of *Flora* margarine which was, according to the newest research, what would protect you from heart attacks. On this he would spread for each slice a triangle of soft cheese, unwrapping it carefully from its silver foil crinkled at the edges and its triangular label. The segments were sold in a small circular flat box—six triangles, arranged in exactly the same space-saving way as a peewit's clutch, their points facing inwards, their curved outer edges forming a segment of the circle's perimeter. He learned to chew slowly, relishing and making the most of every mouthful. There was no way out of eating what his mother made for him, except by eating smaller amounts, but sometimes he would just tell her he'd already eaten, especially if she came in late from the Bingo, which was her one solitary extravagance: the numbers pored over, the potential of winning some unearned amount, a hundred pounds, or even two hundred, the shouted 'House!' She would return with tales of who had won this or that like a sailor returning from a distant tropical island recounting episodes of enviable good fortune which were almost never hers. One memorable night she won a hundred pounds. He was given a crisp, new £10 note, a windfall from a windfall. When his mother was out at the bingo his father would sit in the semi-darkness with all the lights off, on the hard chair beside the table with its leaves folded down, a can of Tennent's lager on its narrowed surface, a young, smiling, attractive woman in a photograph printed convexly around one half of the tall cylinder. The flickering images from the TV screen, invisible in the corner as you came in the front door, ghosted across his father's face and across the room until it was time for him to fetch Jed's mother again—a space for thirty minutes in which the boy could delve undisturbed in the kitchen. The conversation now with his father was simple grunts and sullen acknowledgements. His father did not like him, though he did not care about this. At least it was predictable. He had birds. If he ever complained about anything, such as the light going on in the kitchen when he was trying to sleep, the response was: 'If you don't like it, move out.' But he had no money to move out. He was caught. Sometimes he would fantasise about simply walking off and not coming back.

★

Another facet of his interest in birds and what he could do in relation to them had opened to him that winter. He had become interested in where they slept at night, how they roosted. There seemed little information available about this, even in his big AA book, and as an activity it had the perverse advantage of taking him out of the only place he could comfortably be himself, his bedroom, and breaking up the boredom of the long winter nights before bed.

He would take the big red blocky torch with its white carrying handle and its powerful beam, the one that took the brickish solid rectangular battery, from the cupboard where it was kept in the kitchen and smuggle it out under his heavy coat, and he would wander. The frosty nights were the best: there was no possibility of getting rained on and the night world was still, all the twigs and remnant foliages glitteringly rimed in the stark yellow electric beam of the torch as he swung it from bush to bush or skywrote his name among the constellations, swooping it with easy power across the dark like a bird. The world around the caravan site was different at night. It was full of otherness and silence, transformed by the torchbeam. He would take the track down through the coppiced hazels to the river valley and walk along it, swinging the beam across the twigs and branches and tree trunks and cross the stilled fields, his wellingtonned feet crunching the frosty grass, and swoop back with the torch beam, like a guard in a conning tower with a searchlight in a film, if he thought he had spotted something interesting. Once or twice he entered the sitka spruce plantation at the top of the witchwood. But the closely clustered trees, with their peculiarly scratchy twigs that raked across his face as he passed, and the sudden silence as he padded over the frost-free beds of spruce needles on the forest floor, were too strange and claustrophobic even for him.

PLATE 5.

Otherwise, he felt little sense of the sinister on these night walks. The sinister was human.

He had read that little groups of finches would often roost in favoured spots, especially among ivy. Ivy was good because it was leaf cover in the winter and helped to keep them warm. Sometimes he would startle blackbirds and thrushes sitting among the thorns deep in a bush: the delicate speckling on the breast of a thrush in the brilliant light among all the spikes. He would flick the torch beam off so as not to blind it or disturb it further: the whole night sky again, suddenly given back. This bird or that—a fieldfare or a redwing, wintering thrushes from the arctic he could tell by their cries (a 'chack-chack' for a fieldfare, a thin, high 'see-app' for a redwing)— would rocket out of a hedge with a thick, feathery whirr and simply fly out, among constellations, into the night air, somewhere, sometimes momently highlit to brilliance by the swinging of his torch beam as he tried to track the bird's flight.

He had read that some passerines roosted in little tree holes and crannies. In the ash tree on the edge of the ridge he would walk along, before ascending the last field slope to the caravan site, he discovered, high up inside a hole in the trunk, the black-and-white tail feathers, the thin, scaly legs and feet, of a great tit roosting. It was there every time he checked. He read that treecreepers sometimes scooped out little hollows in the soft spongy bark of wellingtonia trees and used them to roost in. One day he checked the trunk of the big wellingtonia that sat in the middle of the caravan site and swayed and made a swishing

PLATE 6

sound in the wind at night as you passed it while the branches of the yews around clacked against each other like bones. Sure enough, there were little scoops out of the bark. He went back on the first frosty night and flicked on the beam of the torch. There it was, shivering minutely, the head and small curved beak tucked into the back: a little ball of astonishingly detailed brown and startling-white feather. He could have touched it, but he knew better. He flicked the beam off, and gave it back to the frosty dark and the constellations.

There was a sense of breathless excitement to him when he came back into the caravan from these night frost-walks. The blood glittered around his body and his chilled hands and feet slowly returned to warmth in the little bedroom. He was alive with the power of being fifteen. The frosty night and all its sleeping birds across the dark countryside were a welcoming space for him. There they all were, as he was, curled in his bed: a passerine sheltering in its cranny, but without wings.

★

That Christmas he had read a book about the famous bird photographer Eric Hosking, one of the best known in the world. 'My maternal grandfather insisted that he was not a butcher. A meat purveyor, yes: a butcher, no;' it began. Hosking had taken bird photographs all over the world, including almost every British species at the nest. Jed had seen his name as photographer in a book called *Nesting Birds and their Eggs* and had grown curious. The front cover of Hosking's autobiography had a large black and white photograph of a Tawny Owl, perched on the rim of a tree hole, a mouse in its talons. Among many other things the book told the story about this owl: it had made Hosking famous. He had been adjusting flash equipment in a tree beside the tree the owl was nesting in when it swooped out of the dark and plunged the talons of one foot into an eye. He lost the sight of the eye and when he got out of hospital the first thing he did was go back again and shoot the owl—on film. Its photograph, published worldwide, earned many thousands of pounds and was one of the defining events of Eric Hosking's life. He was the man who had cared so much about birds and photography that he'd gone back and photographed the bird that had taken his eye out. The title of his autobiography was: *An Eye For a Bird*.

Jed's *AA Book of British Birds* had touched briefly on bird photography. Like everything else, such as birdwatching and nest recording, it was a whole world with its star performers unknown to the public but famous on the 'scene'. Taking photographs was another form, a less harmful one, of collecting. It was the same instinct, the same desire of wanting to possess something that you loved, or to replicate it in some way. To get close to birds without them knowing you were there was the great thing. One of the easiest ways of doing this involved something these winged creatures of freedom were attached to biologically: their nest. He was learning there was a whole tradition of photographs of birds at the nest, sitting on eggs and feeding young: a whole intimate panoply of images of passerines, say, blackbirds or thrushes, thrusting beaks crammed and coiled with worm meat, moths and craneflies, deep into the gaping maws of nestlings yearning upwards on their scrawny necks: *Feed me! Feed me!* The vital voracity of the natural world.

Jed developed a desire to belong, too, to this subculture. But first he needed a hide—a small canvas tent the size of a portable toilet. He found in a bird magazine that the gold standard for these was 'the Fensman', made out of camouflaged khaki, complete with metal poles and a carrying bag, but it was out of his budget, as most things were, without the wonders of hire purchase. There were no Fensman hides in his mother's catalogue. So he had to make his own, with some canvas he bought in the *Exchange & Mart* and some fence posts he'd purloined from a fencing job in the landscape. Someway or other he'd cut and folded and gathered the big length of heavy lime-green canvas so that with much red-faced struggling it could be draped over the four thick fence stobs, which had to be hammered into the ground, the whole making an optimistic re-enactment of the streamlined lightweight perfection of 'the Fensman', though his hide settled into all sorts of unmanageable heavyweight folds under which he disappeared as under a too-large blanket, half-suffocated by the weight of the heavy material smelling strongly of new canvas. He would peer through the raggedy slit he had made in the hide's 'front' in imitation of the graceful lens turret of the Fensman.

There were various practical limitations to this arrangement. The Fensman, like a one-man tent, rolled up and folded away into a practical small package for easy carrying. Jed, on the other hand, had to make two trips with his homemade hide, one to carry the fence posts, two under each arm, their sharpened tips pointing ahead, in a parody of a medieval knight galloping out, lance a-tilt, onto the jousting field. This was a tiring procedure as the individual posts in each pair did not seem always to want to retain their parallel duality; one or other kept tilting at an odd angle and pointed earthward or skyward so he would have to stop and readjust them before proceeding to the erection point, through whatever woods or across whatever landscape. He would then repeat the journey with the canvas, folded up as well as possible, spilling out of his arms, filling his nostrils with its peculiar reek. The recalcitrant nature of the physical world. This hide was a perfect example of the clash of strong desire, impracticality and no money. 'Patience and persistence, Ger'd,' his mother would say to him, 'will take a snail to Jerusalem.' He wasn't entirely clear what this meant but he would not be deterred and this head-down, brow-to-the -universe, attitude was a gift of a sort.

One spring, the moorhen he sometimes watched, flicking comically along under the banking on the opposite side of the Annick Water, had begun building its nest on boulders that the river, sunk to a low point in the dry weather, had exposed: a little platform on which it sat, motionless, incubating its eggs: a perfect opportunity to try out his hide, as he could erect it on the riverbank where the latter abutted the wood, just above the nest.

All he needed was a camera. He hadn't one himself, but a neighbour whose grass he cut had one. Jed had taken a little 'introduction to photography' guide out of the library. It was a new world to learn, all over again. He asked the neighbour, choosing his moment carefully, if he could borrow his little camera. He knew it was not exactly what he needed. That was a 'single lens reflex', which had a 'pentaprism', which bent the light coming through the lens and bounced it out through the little window at the back of the 'viewfinder' that you looked through to take the photograph. These were the best because they let you see exactly what you were photographing. This kind of camera also took different lenses and what he needed was a telephoto—the lens equivalent of a telescope attached to the camera. He did not have either of those but his neighbour said he could borrow his little camera. It was a 'rangefinder' with an ordinary lens. You peered into the little window, turned the focusing ring to focus it, and in the viewfinder two images of the object you were looking at moved closer together in a little yellowish square in the middle. When the two merged and became one, the object was in focus and you could take the picture.

Everything—all this—could have been told to him quite plainly in fifteen minutes by someone who knew about the world of cameras. But he did not know anyone who did. He delved in the introduction to photography like the boy who'd ventured out looking for roosting birds in the night-time woods.

On the appointed day he had crept down through the woods above the riverbank and ducked in through the back of the 'hide', which he had erected, saggily, on the bank above the moorhen's nest. The canvas reek was strong, but not unpleasant. The canvas lay in folds all around him; it sagged on his head. The closeness of the canvas and the sounds of his breath and the slight scraping sounds his arms made against the material as he moved seemed magnified in the close confines of the little chamber. He squinted down through the ragged window he'd cut in the front of the hide. There was the nest, seeming rather distant, built up of straws on the boulders whitened by the sun, about a third of the way across the river, but with no bird sitting on it.

He had forgotten he would need something to sit on, so he had to kneel. The dampish ground among the club-rush on the floor of the hide seeped through the material of his jeans and made two dark patches, one on each knee. To be at the right angle to look out, he had to kneel up straight as he sometimes did in the pew in chapel; to rest and get some relief from this position he would sink back down so his buttocks as he knelt rested on his heels. There was something claustrophobically exciting about being concealed in the little hide. It was like being under the covers of an unmanageable heavy duvet reading a book by torchlight. He could hear the birds singing at various points out through the wood. That was a wren. Further away, a chaffinch. Behind him, the sudden expostulation of a blackbird—the rush of exclamatory notes ending abruptly.

He raised himself on his knees, straightened his back, and peered through the raggedy slit. At just that moment, the moorhen was approaching the nest from the right, swimming methodically across the stiller water, its tail flicking rhythmically and mechanically. In high excitement he lifted the camera, filled with a fresh roll of film his neighbour had loaded for him, to his eye. The bird seemed further away than it was when he looked at it with his naked eye. He turned the focusing ring and tried to get the two images of it, distant in what seemed another, strangely remote world, and moving across the little window, to merge with each other. This was difficult because the bird was moving, so he pressed the shutter button and hoped for the best. Click. At the sound of the shutter, which seemed loud to him in the hide, the moorhen stopped a moment. He lowered the camera and peeked out. The bird paused, listening, then went on, finally reaching the edge of the little archipelago of boulders the nest was built on, and stepped up and onto the nest.

He quickly learned that an incubating bird did not provide an endless spectacle for a naturalist's notebook. The moorhen sat there, a small dark speck with a waxy red, green and yellow beak, like an unlikely monarch on its little throne built up of straws, almost entirely motionless. Occasionally it would turn on the nest, or stretch its neck out to pick at a short length of straw and lift it, and add it to the edge of the nest. He lifted the camera to his eye a few more times but he already knew with some disappointment that his photographs would not mark the illustrious beginning of his career as a nature photographer. He did not have the necessary equipment. This was his constant dilemma. After about an hour he slipped backwards out of the hide, barely daring to breathe in case the moorhen heard him and, keeping the hide between the bird's line of sight and himself, he stole back up the slope of the witchwood, breathing more easily as he got further away until at the top of the slope he felt liberated from the silence and the cramped, canvas-reeking and strangely intense atmosphere of the hide into space and light and air.

—I don't think my pictures will have turned out, he said to his neighbour.

—Ah. I'll give you them when I develop the rest of the film.

A few weeks later, his neighbour handed him the fifteen or so little prints: the bird was an almost unrecognisable speck in the centre of the frame.

Eric Hosking, though, had started off similarly. Jed's own future plans by the time he finished Hosking's book that winter in the holidays were now starting to involve hides and sitting close to birds for the prize of beautiful images. He began noticing not only bird photographs in books but also the picture credits. Eric Hosking. John Markham. S. C. Bisserot. Arthur Gilpin. Who were all these people, out there in the world?

★

He lay on his back in bed on the Sunday night before the return to school in early January and when
he felt along his upper body with his fingertips the
curved ridges of his ribs stuck up like the struts and
ridges of some ship buried in sand and half-revealed
by a storm. The great bones of his pelvis felt huge
and powerful. He imagined himself as a skeleton
glowing greenly in the dark, stretched over with
flesh. And then, with the rest of his family, he was
asleep under the constellations flickering frostily
above the nighttime Ayrshire landscape. The lanes
went off out there, shining whitely and bare in the
moonlight. Owls threw out their quavering calls in
the far woods of Annick Lodge. The coals in the
stove in the caravan living room, backed up for the
night by his father, collapsed a little and resettled
into a new position.

He felt strange going back to school, as if he was
attending it for the first time. He had had eight
weeks of his own routine involving the floodpool
at Warwickdale, the world of Eric Hosking, tawny
owls, and bird photographers with one eye, and
nighttime adventures with a flashlight looking for
roosting birds. Now he was back to timetables, his
few schoolfriends, and the terrifying complexities
of girls in all their exotic plumages and mocking
laughters. But something had happened. He was
now so light and fasted and airy that he did not sin
very often at night anymore and was instead so tired
he fell asleep instead. Looking at the girls, and their
dazzling differences, he no longer felt threatened
by the desire rising in himself at their closeness. It

was as if he were regarding them from a distance, in another dimension, or as if he were a spectator at a play, not one of the actors, as everyone else was. The hot blood rarely sprang to his face at a dropped word or a glimpse any more.

With those differences, by midday on that first Monday morning, it was as if he had not had an absence at all. At lunchtime in the bleak January midday grey, he walked the High Street as usual, and spent a half hour in the town library in the county building at the Cross reading Gayelord Hauser's *Guide to Intelligent Reducing* in its perfectly ordered world where bad things never happened to anyone. On other days he would take the harbour walk, where winter redshanks and curloos flickered across the dark exposed mud of the River Irvine at the estuary, but he felt the cold more now, especially in frosty weather. He had shifted from finding himself overheating in classrooms and presenting his beacon face to the world to being glad of their warmth. Warmth became a refuge now that to some degree he had lost his fear of girls. He had outwitted their power over him. He was no longer, except rarely, hiding what he thought in his bed late at night because there was nothing to be hidden. Girls sat on their pedestals, Virgin-Mary-like, observing with a vague disinterest and distaste as he thought the snorting debauched lusts of their worshippers, the teenage boys. Now he was the girls' equal. In another school, years before, he had written a ludicrous story involving King Kong and an aeroplane crash—the ground around the crash site 'soaked with blood'—which for some reason baffling to him had won some prize at the school. To his trembling horror, he had been summoned out of the anonymous rows of the school assembly up onto a stage, where he had to read his story, under a light, from a podium. He shuffled, panicking, down the central aisle of the hall, and turned left along the front row of pupils to ascend the stage clutching his handwritten story. The row consisted entirely of girls. As he passed along it, like a wave marking his progression or a wind through a line of summer trees they each recoiled, drawing up their knees, making little mock groans and squeals of disgust. There was something wrong with boys, or with him. These things proved it.

★

His happy, holy and sexless state did not last long. Slowly over the next few months he began eating more again. Sometimes on a freezing day of an east wind down at the harbour he would have the outrageous luxury of a Scotch pie with its grey meats and its running melted lard hotly coating his fingers: a little point of heat, like a speck of sun, in the vast cold, burning his wind-numbed fingertips. And with his appetite came back his desire. Occasionally on his walks he would discover some discarded magazine at a verge, exciting as a rare bird's nest, and there would follow several days of frenzy when he stored it like a casket in some cranny in a ruined building webby and musty with mould in ironic contrast to the sumptuous sets and the silk and the satin where perfect women liked men and boys. But this would only last for a few days and then he would have to destroy the evidence, throwing it over a bridge into some wood where he could not find it again, before it incinerated him with its incandescence. He would then begin the long climb back up the peak of purity where the regression to his bestial nature had never happened. *Numenius arquata, Anas crecca, Falco columbarius, Phalacrocorax aristotelis, Corvus corax*, the Latin names gone through like beads in a rosary, a frail counter against the energy of the Universe powering itself through his blood. He was once more that farmhand armed with a scythe against the Iliadic and tautly-muscled might of Achilles, tamer of horses. He stood there wielding the ritualistic Latin like a bin lid for a shield.

PLATE 12.

★

The astonishment of occupying, or being, a body. A point was reached in his recovery from the weight loss of the winter, a perfect point when he was completely in equilibrium between lightness and heaviness. Sometimes he would walk ten or twenty miles a day at weekends or in school holidays. He went on a school sponsored walk one smirry Friday along Irvine shore to Troon—the whole school year, tramping through mizzle on a dreich mild winter Friday, along the front at Irvine Harbour—and wasn't that a winter-plumaged red throated diver in the Irvine, near the river mouth?—and then the long relief and unrestricting space of the shoreline and the figures who had started earlier disappearing, far off, in trails, in the rain mist. Gaggles of excited youngsters, lively as winter greylags, one group paused in a little huddle around something on the beach, one toeing it tentatively—a dead porpoise, half-buried in sand. The great otherness of the sea, constant on the shore, collapsing in little tangles of white and cream, withdrawing again down the gleam of wet sand darted and sprinted across by small waders: dunlin, sanderling, redshank. The whole school year had to walk to the rocks at Barassie, then turn around and retrace their steps. Already those who had set off later were meeting the earlier groups on their return journeys. There was something happy about the space and the smirr and the grey-green of the Firth. It was big enough to accommodate all his thoughts. They could be lost

WHITE-FRONTED GOOSE

PURRE OR DUNLIN

in it, insignificant as a single sandgrain on the long beach curving around the bay. On the way back, near the end of this walk, which took them several hours, something happened. He ran the last short section, up the slope at the Low Green, back to the school, and his running seemed to him effortless, as if he was gliding, or made of light, and not this system of pumps, muscles, ligaments and sinew heavy with the weight of earth.

He had dreams of elegance, not in any fashionable sense but in being wholly at ease in his body, wholly adjusted to the landscape, like a poised athlete of the woods. He remembered the Marvel comics of his childhood—Thor with his hammer, Mjolnir; the character Namor, Lord of Atlantis, with his superb physique, perfect slicked-back hairline, and the little wings on his ankles which served some unlikely purpose never explained but which looked good. Namor could only be out of the water for three hours before starting to lose his great strength. From these early comics Jed had learned big words: *Behemoth. Leviathan. Amulet.* This last belonged to one of his favourite characters, Dr Strange, in his flamboyant cloak with its stiff, raised collar. He had particular positions for his fingers and hands when he was casting spells. Jed had mimicked these as a wee boy. If the black-and-white TV picture suddenly dissolved in a blizzard of snow-static, he would focus and try and use his mental powers to bring the picture back, his fingers angled as would have been Dr Strange's. It did not work, of course, or at least not often enough for him to attribute it to his own magic powers rather than chance.

What was left to him in his mid-teens were dreams of hunter-gatherer perfect self-sufficiency. His fitness was a part of this. He would do pull-ups on the lateral branch of a yew tree on the caravan site positioned at exactly the right height. Ten; fifteen. He admired the veins in his biceps—one thick blue one, crossed laterally by a thinner vein. A friend of his in gym class in the changing room had veins running across the tops of his arms and the front of his shoulders below his clavicles. Jed admired these enormously and coveted something similar for his own physiology. He took to moving through the woods in the spring lightly and carefully, watching for the danger of crackable twigs underfoot. He had a small canvas shoulder bag for his weekend expeditions: the cheese sandwiches wrapped in silver foil that crinkled around them and bendable into whatever shape; he took care not to leave any of the white bread exposed to the air and so in danger of drying out. The digestive biscuits, similarly wrapped. An apple or two, hopefully crisp and tangy and sizzling to the bite and tongue, not soft and yielding. He needed his teeth to break off crisp, dense fragments, bright and jagged and alive with juice. A flask, full of good hot tea, steam upwising in the winter wood, his chilled hands curled around the little cap-cup. These small things gave him great pleasure.

The previous summer an Irish uncle had shown him how to set a wire snare for rabbits for the pot,

how to make the running slipknot in the snare so
that as it tightened the rabbit strangled itself. You
found out where the rabbits had their runs, say below a fence, and set the snare there. In the valley below the caravan site there were lots of rabbits, lol-
loping around at the edge of the hedges. He found
a track below the lowest wire strand of a fence into
what had been the back garden of the white ruined
cottage, near where the great tits nested in the water pump every spring. He set his snare here, dan-
gling its open loop, its 'O' of thin metal from the
lowest strand of the fence so it was at rabbit height,
and left it.

The first time he came back to check, there was a
rabbit in it, pulling and tugging this way and that.
His reaction was of sheer horror. He put both his
palms on the furry soft back of the wide-eyed animal
to pin it to the ground and stop it strangling itself
further in trying to escape. Keeping it pinned with
such force with one hand that it would not sense any
weakness and so struggle by being encouraged by the
lightening of pressure, he searched with the fingers
of his right hand for where the loop of the snare had
tightened, buried in fur, around the animal's neck.
With the force of desperation he managed to loop
the point of his little finger just under the edge of
the wire and loosen it a little—enough to give him
purchase and open a wider gap and start to reverse
the loop from the full stop it had been constricting
to around the animal's neck back to the open 'O'
it was originally. He managed to loosen it and slip
it open, releasing the deadly wire from round the

windpipe of the terrified, wide-eyed creature, and slip it over its head and its big ears that were pulled forward over its brow by the forward motion of the wire. He lifted his left hand from its back. It sat a second, gazing in astonishment, then sprinted away.

He did not want to think of the panicked animals's hapless self-stranglement under the wire that, the more it struggled, the tighter the wire grew. At the same time he was impressed that it had worked and that he had snared a rabbit. But he never set another snare.

★

Winter into spring: the first song thrushes—'*Spring is coming! Spring is coming! So I sing! So I sing!*'—sang from vantages at the top of buildings or trees. He noticed them as he noticed everything to do with birds. Not a strange bird could chirrup, sing or cry but he wanted to know what it was. The first song thrushes were like the first stars coming out in a night that would soon be full of them.

He went back to his mother's catalogue, flicking through it. His attention had now shifted to another new world to discover: cameras. All that glinting technology at insane prices far beyond him so, as usual, he looked at what was possible based on how much he would have to pay per week of the two options of 26 weeks or 52. He had worked out that for bird photography he needed an SLR that took interchangeable lenses. There were two budgetary possibles, both from Russia—the Zenit B and the

PLATE 4

GOLDEN ORIOLE.

Zenit E. They were more or less the same except the 'E' had a built-in light meter. He read up about lenses. These cameras came with a standard lens of 50mm which corresponded to the perspective and magnification of the human eye. But if he was going to photograph birds he needed, he learned, a telephoto. Each extra 50mm in lens length added 100% magnification. So 100mm was x2; 200mm, x4; 300mm, x6. The books recommended 135mm for photographing birds at the nest, but he wanted also to photograph them elsewhere. So he chose an Optomax 300mm with a screw thread mount that would fit the camera. It was a budget lens as the Zenit E was a budget camera, though his instinct even then was to choose the very best he could afford for anything he cared about, aspiring as he did to perfection and order, in that activity at least; for the rest, the world could have been collapsing round him and he would barely have noticed.

He had saved some money given at Christmas and the previous late summer had had a stroke of luck when he'd been walking the lane on the way to Fairliecrevoch and Malcolm Wilson's wife, blonde and Nordic, was clopping past on her horse. She stopped beside him, and the great smooth convex flanks of the animal flexed a little as it breathed.

—You're from the caravan site aren't you?

—Yes.

—How would you like to earn some money? she said. —We need help getting the hay in.

—I'd like that.

—Go along to the farm. I'll tell Malcolm you're coming.

It was a long weekend. All across the fields around Fairliecrevoch the balers had been working, disgorging from their rear ends, like the methodically produced droppings of some great metal insect as it progressed, the rectangular hay bales bound with twine. Hundreds and hundreds of them. There was a rush on to get the hay in in the good weather to stop it being spoiled or having to sit in the field till it was dry enough to bring in without its rotting in the barn.

He was put to work in the barn at first with two other men, the men standing up at the top of the stack of hay to build it. His job was to feed the conveyor with bales off the back of the trailer to keep the two men up there supplied. He was so ignorant at first that, among the clanking and juddering of the conveyor, ridged across every three feet or so, as the belt moved round he placed the bales laterally on the conveyor so each end hung out over its edge. The bales simply rolled back down, hitting his calves with the weight of incompetence. One of the men at the top gestured over the deafening noise of the conveyor how to place the bales correctly: lengthwise, and so the bottom edge was supported by the ridge across the conveyor. Jed was flame-faced with embarrassment in the hot still air of the barn that slowly ovened in the sunlight. These small moments, taken together, built up to everything. There was a right way to do everything. Sometimes the wrong way also worked, though it did not here. When he found the right way, to impress the men at the top with his eagerness and so he would not be sacked for his earlier ineptness, he went into bale-loading frenzy. He was soon rivering with sweat in the dry airlessness and heat of the barn. The two men at the top found themselves subjected to such a barrage of bales being dumped off the conveyor at the top they could not stack and place them quick enough; soon they stood waist high among the irregularly angled blocks of dried summer grass. They gestured at him to slow down, one man miming a horizon line with a lateral motion of his downturned palms, each slicing out from the other to an imagined edge.

One of the men switched off the conveyor and the rotating belt slowed to a stop. Silence. 'Mon up,' he shouted down.

Jed climbed up the cliff face of hay to help them. It was easier than climbing trees. There were lots of purchases, small divots where you could thrust your feet into the gaps between the bales and curling your fingers round the baler twine that bound them all, feeling its thin length cutting into your fingers and palms. So he stood, up in the heights of the roof where the heat was more intense and the two men sat resting on the edges of bales, their breaths slowing, rivulets of sweat, like rain down a window pane, on their foreheads. He sat with them in the reassuring airless stillness. He barely took a deeper breath. In these moments, he was entirely his body. He did not need anything else. He was immortal.

Malcolm Wilson seemed a very different man and farmer from Davy Smith. For one thing, he was huge, 6 foot six inches tall at least, and affirming.

—You're a good worker, Jed.

Mealtimes here were affairs of sheer abundance, and there were lots of breaks for coffee and tea, all in the big kitchen of the farmhouse. It was accepted that the men were sweating and throwing bales around and that they should eat accordingly. And because they worked into the evening, supper was included as well.

It was 9pm that night before he got home with all his limbs stiff and a glow of heat and food on him, his clothes speckled and dusty with hay. He lay in the little bedroom. All night the planet turned and the sun moved along the north, below the horizon in the direction of the witchwood, like some great sunken animal. His dreams were full of golden bales.

The whole weekend, and the Monday, was like this: great physical exertion, a licence to eat too much food, stiff limbs, a rush to get the bales in. He felt the weight of physicality in the world, the horror and terror of the material. It was what there was. That first night he had expected to be paid for his day's work. There was a pause as he stood at the door of the kitchen, awkwardly. Malcolm Wilson was just discussing something with another worker at the big kitchen table, an older man.

—I'm just wondering if I get paid, he said, into a brief silence.

—We pay you at the end, Jed, Wilson said, not unkindly. When the job's finished.

—He went away and the idea of how much he might get paid led to all sorts of speculations, from the merely standard, such as the £2 a day he'd received from Davy Smith to the possibility of an unexpected largesse, such as £4 a day. The idea of this payment was a vague enticing eventuality, like the thought of an unusual bird in a wood.

It was Monday, late afternoon. They had been out in the field, building the last bales into a stack on the back of the trailer. He had quickly learnt the knack of this—the bales were twice as long as they were wide, so you could stack them in symmetrical towers. His body had grown used to the lugging, the hooking of the fingers under the baler twine that bound each one, the rubbing of the twine against your callused palms, the deadweight of each bale, some heavier than others, but not so heavy it hurt to lift it, the swinging round with it to face the trailer, the hoisting of it, using one knee for leverage under it to raise it to the level of your chest and heave it with all your strength as high as you could so the person on the trailer had less height of air to pull it up through.

They came in at last, sitting high on the swaying bales, seeing everything, the whole sweep of fields, the clock in the farm tower at Girgenti Farm, the Moss where the curloos and snipe nested, from this new aspect. Dark clouds were building on the horizon. The yellow fields were stripped and bare of bales, denuded with a look that sheep had when their fleeces have been shorn in the spring. The tractor driver drove gently so as not to teeter the top bales but now and then a divot or hole in the field swayed them at an unusual angle so Jed gripped a bale by its twine for balance.

He was paid in the house after mugs of tea and

JACK SNIPE

digestive biscuits when the last load had been stored in the barn's dry, hay-smelling airlessness. Malcolm Wilson handed him twenty-five pounds. He was astonished but was careful not to show it.

—Will you come out again if we need you?

—Yes.

He went home exhilarated. His other way of earning money at that time was mowing the neighbours' grass and tidying their gardens on the caravan site. He took a special pride in the neatness of the mowing and was paid two pounds per garden. He was always looking for ways to combine work with physical exercise.

So it was that he had a little money to start paying for the Zenit E camera and the Optomax lens from his mother's catalogue. He had to order them some weeks apart or his mother would have been alarmed

at his profligacy and worried in case he defaulted on
his weekly payments. He ordered the camera first.
The Zenit E was a big heavy clunker of a camera,
functional but inelegant. Even he could see that. To
load it you swung open the back, placed the film
canister into position, pulled out the long tongue
of narrow film from the canister's slot and wound,
with the camera's wind-on lever, this leading edge
around the sprockets of the metal rod that wrapped
the exposed film around itself. The film canister
was anchored on the other side of the film gate
that the film crossed for each exposure. The wind-
on lever, with a satisfying buzzy sound, pulled the
next segment of unexposed film to its position in
the film gate. When you reached the end of the film
after 36 frames, you rewound the film back across
the film gate into its canister with the rewind lever,
which was on the opposite side of the camera from
the wind-on lever. The film was safe, then, rolled
up in the dark of the light-tight canister. It was
your life, stored away and untouchable. It could
then be developed.

After several weeks he ordered the Optomax
300mm lens. This was a big development—he
peered through it into the 'ground glass' viewfinder,
dim and documentary, of the Zenit E. He then discovered that he would need a tripod if he was going
to photograph birds at the nest. To his amazement,
he discovered that his father had one, stored in a cupboard and left over from his home-movie days with
super-8 cine cameras, now hardly used—bought
at some period of aspiration and long forgotten. It

was shoogly and not perfect, but it held the camera with the big lens attached to the front. He then discovered further—this seemed to be a characteristic of photography, that one item of equipment then needed another—that he should have a cable release, which was basically a little cable that screwed into the shutter-release button and had a plunger at the end, with two little metal brackets you curved your first and second fingers around while you depressed the plunger gently with your thumb to release the shutter. The camera's mirror would then flip up inside the camera body, and a little vertical slit in the fabric of the shutter would flick across the film gate, exposing that frame of the film to light. Without the cable release, if you pressed the shutter button with your finger you could cause vibration so the picture would be blurred if you couldn't use a fast enough shutter speed. He learnt that three things in photography were in relation to each other—the shutter speed; the lens aperture, indicated by numbers: f5.6, f.11, etc, which governed the amount of light the lens admitted; and the ASA 'speed' of the film, which marked its sensitivity to light. The faster the shutter speed, the less light it let in. The lower the aperture the more light the lens let in. The higher the ASA the more sensitive the film was to light. These three facets were in a constant dance together. The aim was to get the correct amount of light to the little rectangle of silver halide that was the film frame for the perfect exposure. But he was learning too about all the complications and trade-offs necessary. The lower the film speed, the higher the quality of the image. The slower the shutter speed, the higher the likelihood of either 'camera shake'—blurring through the camera's movement—or movement from the subject of the photograph. The lower the aperture, the less, laterally, of the subject, from front to back, would be in focus. All these matters he had to grasp if he wanted to photograph birds at the nest, and all were centred on light. Light was king.

The world of photography was like an extensive forest full of increasing intricacy that he stood only at the edge of. It was a whole other world of experience and awareness but it had a big disadvantage compared to the simple world of just looking at the birds themselves: you needed money. No sooner had you bought one new item than you discovered you needed another which was necessary either because you'd bought the first thing or because what you wanted to do couldn't be achieved without it. The best equipment for him was simply impossible in the world of photography with its topflight Nikons, Canons, Minoltas, Asahi Pentaxes, Contaxes, Leicas, Hasselblads, the lenses marvellous circles in the advertising photographs with their glass elements reflecting a world of ideal precision and detail. Photography was a way of making a stilled, lifeless beauty out of the everyday flux and chaos and grief of life, and its appeal was felt fully by Jed, caught up as he was in the little bedroom with his father monitoring his every move in the kitchen.

He was now looking at the bird photographs in the books wondering what lens they had used, what camera, what flash. Some of the latest photographers like Stephen Dalton were specialising in high-speed flash photography—astonishing images of blue tits, kingfishers, starlings or swallows in flight, frozen in a 1/30,000th of a second micro-slice of time. It would be many years before he would find these eerie and strangely clinical in their absolute perfection and not something to aspire to. To emulate them would have taken hundreds of pounds worth of equipment and also the entire infrastructure—access to the birds, time, the best cameras and lenses—to set it all up. His reality was different.

One wet miserable Saturday he took the green single-decker bus the fourteen miles to Ayr from the lane end of the drive. He had taken to looking in large newsagents at the range of camera magazines—most of them packed with advertisements and discounts and supposed bargains, each magazine as subtly different as species in a family of passerines. And all their equipment usually involving sums of money, hundreds of pounds, inconceivable to him. Money was marvellous. It could change itself into expensive camera gear as surely as it in turn could change itself into all the bird photographs in the nature books.

It was a miserable late-winter day. A steady rain had set in, miles and miles of unrelieved grey with its weight of Atlantic water drifting in onto the coast from the Firth of Clyde—soaking the white gannets of Ailsa Craig and the Saturday shoppers in the busy town shuffling in crowds under umbrellas. The front cover of *SLR Camera* that month, just out, had a compelling picture of lenses on the cover

KINGFISHER.

PLATE 26.

with a strapline: 'The Lens Guide for Perfect Photographs.' For some reason, flicking through the issue,
Jed began convincing himself that if he didn't buy
it, he would have missed the one chance in which
he could become a nature photographer; the gleaming, violet-glassed optics of the lenses on the cover
held the promise of magnificently sharp images in
diamonding light; a perfect world.

There was a problem. He had fifty pence. The
magazine cost fifty pence. The cost of his bus ticket
home was also fifty pence. For some reason he had
not bought a return. He had to choose either the
magazine or the bus ticket. He went out of the shop
and walked the crowded, jostling streets, a chaos of
umbrellas, shopping bags, girning youngsters and
harassed parents, while he considered this dilemma.
The issue of *SLR Camera*, without which his life
would be entirely different, brightened in import
in his mind until he knew that if he did not have it
some vital piece of knowledge that meant the suc-
cess of all his future photographic endeavours would
be lost. He would be shown to himself as not serious
enough; a failure. He wrestled with this thought, returning to the newsagents several times, taking the
magazine down, looking at it, walking out into the
street again.

Finally he took the copy off the shelf, went to the
counter, and handed over his fifty pence.

—Would you like it in a bag?

—Yes please.

When he got to the shop door, he tucked the
magazine in its bag below his left arm under his coat,

zipped it up, and walked out into the street turning not left, to the bus station, but right, along Ayr High Street. He took the road past the Carnegie Library, and began to walk. By the time he reached the outskirts of the town the constant rain had started to seep through the acrylic material of his coat. It began to get dark. He had to shift the position of the magazine from under his arm which was growing sore from the pressure he had to exert to stop the magazine slipping under his coat and falling to the ground. Instead, he folded it laterally, once, and thrust the bottom edge down the front of his trousers so he could at least walk unimpeded.

For three and a half hours it rained. On the dual carriageway the cars roared past him, hissing up rainwater in smoky clouds. At one point he grew alarmed when it seemed the rain had seeped through the top edge of the plastic bag that held the magazine and had softened the corners of the precious publication. The rain had now soaked through all his outer garments. He began squelching in his shoes.

It was after eight pm, almost four hours later, when he turned into the drive at the bottom of the caravan site. As if it had punished him enough—it was sometimes difficult not to think of weather as in some way punitive and a character in its own right— the rain slackened. A few stars glinted out between cloud breaks. He was completely sodden, but the precious magazine was safe. He pulled it from under his coat. He took the short route back to his parents' caravan, crossing what had been in more genteel times the tennis court for the big house at Cunning-hamhead, now long grassed-over and used by the summer children for playing football or other games.

He walked down the path, up the caravan steps, and went inside. His mother, it was plain, was out at the Bingo. On the left in the living room, his father sat in his usual favoured spot before the television, the lights off, the glow of the cathode tube and its moving figures playing across the set face like light underwater.

—Where's mum?

—Bingo.

Ordinarily he would have waited till his father left to fetch his mother at around nine-thirty before going into the kitchen to look for food. But he was hungry. He put the magazine into his bedroom, laying it on the bed and unfolding it, took off all his sodden clothes, and pulled on dry jeans and a t-shirt. The dry clothes against his skin, and the dryness itself, were a luxury after the constant drumming rain. His legs were stiff and aching with the fourteen tramped miles in them.

Bread and cheese in the kitchen—a staple. He would take nothing more elaborate as it would increase the complication of the endeavour and the time he spent there and the likelihood of his father bothering him. His father, it seemed, could not just let him be. As soon as Jed flicked the light switch, and the fluorescent tube flickered on after a few half-hearted attempts over the kitchen table with its extra leaf open and propped up, his father would also come into the kitchen. He had a strange wheezing

presence, a remnant of twenty-five years of smoking and childhood asthma.

Jed was buttering the white bread on the plate.
He had taken the cheese out of the fridge and was
slicing it for the sandwich.

—Don't you be takin too much of that cheese. It's
for my lunch tomorrow.

He said nothing but began slicing the cheese more
thinly, and when the kettle clicked off poured the
hot water into the teabag in the mug, added the
milk, and pressed the tea bag against the mug's side
with the spoon. The tea pressed out in a concentrated brown, darkening the milky liquid.

The two sandwiches on a plate in one hand, the
mug in the other, he hooked his socked toes around
the edge of his bedroom door, slid it across on its
runners, put the plate on the bed and the mug on
the floor beside it, closed the door after him, and sat
down, an animal in its lair, and began chewing the
soft white bread. When the coast was clear and his
father had left to pick up his mother he could plun-
der the kitchen again, taking care not to eat anything
which might be missed.

Then his mother would come in in a little flurry
of excitement after her night 'out'—'I only needed a
ten and a three for a hundred pounds tonight!'—and
the kettle would be put on, and the kitchen would
become again a small lit welcoming space, out of the
elements. He saw his mother as wholly good. His father, meanwhile, was a strict, forbidding, grudging
presence who was not able to harm him fully only
because his wife stood in the way. Had Jed been ma-
nipulative he could have used this apparent power he

had with his mother against his father, but he didn't, at least not deliberately. All he wanted was to be left alone. But his mere physical presence seemed an affront to his father.

The copy of *SLR Camera* did not have the significance he had invested it with in the shop. But he had to walk the fourteen miles home in the rain to discover that.

★

He was sitting Highers that spring, but they were not his main interest. *That* was photographing a peewit at the nest in the fields around Cunninghamhead. He had got permission from Malcolm Wilson to put up his hide in a seeded barley field where the birds nested, after explaining to the farmer what was involved. You spent five days moving the hide gradually nearer each day so the bird got used to it. Then when the hide was close enough to the nest to take photographs, someone walked with you to the hide, you slipped inside and set up the equipment, and then the other person walked away. The bird then thought all was safe and would return to the nest. This was supposed to work with birds apart from crows, which could count. Malcolm Wilson was remarkably unperturbed by the idea of his young barley being trodden on. He gave permission freely.

Jed found the nest, the four eggs in their scrape in the ground, lined with a few bits of dried grass, and set the hide up about sixty yards away. Then he watched, hidden in a nearby hedge, to make sure the bird would return to sit on its eggs. The pee-wit picked around among the green barley shoots at first, the slight breeze bending its recurved crest forward over its head as it leant forward—for all the world affecting ignorance that there was a nest to take its interest anywhere nearby. It would edge its way closer, occasionally pausing, tilting its head at the sky and letting out a throaty, uncertain call. As it drew nearer the nest, it began to speed up, and finally cast caution aside in its movement towards the nest. The last ten yards or so were covered in a slightly meandering sprint till it reached the nest, lowered itself, and settled. When Jed lowered his binoculars he could just make out the dark speck on the hillcrest among the whole expanse of feature-less field.

★

The great day came when the hide was close enough to the nest for him to take photographs. The whole process up to that point had made him anxious about weather—wind blowing the hide down, or flapping it too much so that the bird was disturbed by it as by a scarecrow, or heavy rain pooling in what passed for its 'roof' and collapsing the ramshackle canvas. On a few occasions, when he was dismantling it to move the hide forward, the clear night rain that had gathered in its folds and creases splashed over him in a sudden drenching waterfall. *Fuck!* he would say. *Fuck!* He would lie awake at night listening and hoping the wind would not rise, imagining the hide out there in the dark field and the bird sitting.

Because it was exam time he and his school contemporaries were allowed to stay at home to study. He asked a younger boy on the caravan site, after explaining what he was doing, if he would see him to the hide near the nest, walk away afterwards, and come back and fetch him several hours later. The boy was off school with a minor ailment and was enthusiastic. His name was Paul. He was open to everything.

Jed was still learning. The commonly held view among non-photographers was that sunlight out of a blue sky was ideal weather for taking photographs. Now he had read that it was better if it was cloudy but bright. Sunlight simply created a shadow for everything—every blade of grass, every leaf, every spider, every wren or crawling caterpillar, however small, was given its own shadow by the one great star in the sky. And the blue sky of daylight was only space lit by that star, that was just the nearest to them in the Universe, like all the others, distanter, speckling the deep blue-black of the night sky like the dots on a wren's egg. But all those little daytime suncast shadows simply made everything too fussy in photographs, too intricate with light and dark.

The morning they set out for the hide, the tall teenager and the smaller boy, the light was bright but soft. As they approached across the field, in plain sight of the nest so they wouldn't frighten the bird, it left the nest and walked, light-steppingly, away from it, and finally as they approached the hide, which was set up about fifteen feet from the eggs, it took off with a wailing cry.

He lifted the edge of the canvas, bent down, and eased himself into the little square yard-and-a -half of darkness reeking of the thick material. He splayed out the three legs of the tripod, flipped over the small platform for the camera with its bolt with a screw thread, screwed it into the base of the camera, then flipped it horizontal again. The Zenit E, with the great excrescence of the 300mm lens, sat uneasily on this platform. He screwed the cable release into the camera's shutter-release button, then angled the camera lens out through the slit in the canvas and looked through the viewfinder. There was the nest, the four tops of the curved eggs visible in their scrape in the dim graininess of the viewfinder, the miniature window onto another world. The smaller boy, lifting the canvas from behind, a face framed against the brightness and clouds of the ordinary day, watched this whole palaver with interest.

—Can you give me the stool?

Paul handed in the stool they had brought and, angling himself carefully in the cramped space so as not to bump the camera, Jed set it down, shoving its four legs fiercely into the earth to keep it steady, then sat on it. Once he bumped the camera and swung its lens away from the nest, so had to re-angle it again. The stool was slightly too high, but the hide's roof, sagging, was flexible so he could get a little relief from the crick in his neck caused by the squat position he had to adopt by pushing his head up a little into the yielding canvas.

—I think that's me, he said. —Can you watch over at the edge of the field for ten minutes with these binoculars in case I have to signal you to come back? Otherwise just come back and get me at four o'clock.

—Okay.

Paul closed the back flap of the hide, weighting its bottom edge with a few stones to keep it closed.

—I'll see you later, Jed said from inside.

—See you later.

There was the brief sound of Paul walking away, and then he was left in the silence of the hide, in which everything was magnified—the heat, the dark, the sound of his own breathing as the canvas walls pressed in, occasionally rippling a little in a breeze. A skylark sang, somewhere high up, in a cascade of varying twitterings, tiny and particular in the high, wide air. Far away, a tractor growled along a lane. He leant forward and peered through the viewfinder at the framed scene with the curved tops of the eggs surrounded by green barley shoots. It was only a peewit's nest, but to him it was as exciting and beautiful as a Caravaggio to an art connoisseur.

He stared through the viewfinder, aware that he was holding his breath and his face was flushed in the dark of the hide. He waited, tensely expectant. Somewhere out there, beyond his sight, the bird was standing, perhaps staring at the hide in which he was hidden like a thought in a brain, or stepping closer to the nest...

And as he peered, neck-cricked and aware of his

moisture-laden breathing, there was a slight movement in the far upper left of the viewfinder. This
moved at a diagonal down towards the nest in the
foreground, and the blurry green object grew larger
and slowly sharper until there it was, perfectly in focus, his first peewit at the nest, settling over its eggs
and lowering itself onto the clutch. Even in the dim
viewfinder you could make out the bottle-green and
purplish-tinged plumage of its back. It just sat, gazing a little nervily, with one round black eye, at the
hide. Occasionally a breeze rippled the canvas and
the peewit would cock its head, alerted.

He had read that you should wait for some time
after a bird sits on its eggs before trying to take a
photograph. But he was seventeen. He lasted five or
six minutes then, pressing the plunger of the cable
release while he looked through the viewfinder, released the camera shutter. In the close confines and
silence of the hide, the Zenit E's shutter clunked,
seemingly loud as a gunshot. The viewfinder flickered black for an instant, and the bird started on the
nest, alerted from its drowse and peering at the lens.
But after several seconds it settled again and, hardly
daring to breathe, Jed wound on the exposed frame
of film to the next frame, the wind-on lever making
its satisfying slight buzz as he did so.

Throughout the afternoon he repeated this process, taking a picture at intervals, and by the third or
fourth photograph the bird made no response at all
to the clap of the shutter. Halfway through the afternoon she raised herself off the eggs and walked off
the small stage of the viewfinder's theatre, exiting

left. A few minutes later, another bird arrived, suspicious and wary, and settled on the eggs. This bird was darker, more resplendent, with a much longer, more elegant, plume-like crest. It sat proudly upright on the nest, startling afresh at the first clunk of the Zenit shutter. He imagined it must be the male.

And that is how he spent that April afternoon, in a tiny canvas square in the dark, under the wide sky in the broad field, in the Ayrshire landscape around Annick, while kettles were clicking off in farmhouses and the exam-free teenagers were ink-stainedly emerging through the gates at Irvine Royal, and the Arran ferry was rolling through the blue towards Ardrossan, and Janet Donaldson, the school's resident goddess, standing over the toilet bowl, knickers around her knees, was tugging out the blood-soaked tampon by its blue string from between her legs and flushing it down the toilet; he had slowed himself to the pace of a peewit's world, quite beyond timetables, exams, or shops, while the embryos coalesced in the dark of the four eggs under the bird's breast. Not long after, the bird, alerted, cocked its head, and flapped silently off the nest. He drew the canvas at the back of the hide aside. Out in the brightness his small assistant was walking across the field to release him.

—How did it go?

—Great! I think I got pictures of both the male and female.

Back in the safety of his caravan bedroom he very carefully, almost ritualistically, wound the precious exposed film back across the film gate into its little canister, clicked open the back of the camera, pulled up the rewind lever that slotted into the top of the film canister, and plucked out the film as if he were taking an egg from a nest. The images were in there, hidden in the dark. He slipped the film canister into the black plastic container it came in, pressed the plastic cap carefully all round, and slipped it into the envelope addressed to Agfa. They would develop it and send it back as slides, little windows of life mounted in their plastic frames. He would take down the hide the following day. He did not mind what the weather did now.

It was astonishing, the importance he placed on this little canister of images. It was a memorable day, about a week later, when the orange-red plastic box of slides arrived and was waiting for him when he got back up the lane from school. The pictures had turned out! There were the lapwings, sitting on their nest among the barley, but strangely inert and without any glimpse of the eggs, even, to show they were sitting on a nest; but they were his. He slid each slide in turn from the front of the two rows in the box they came in, held it to the light of the sky coming through his bedroom window, examined it, and slotted it down at the back of the row into its box again. It was the not knowing how it would turn out that was exciting. It was like not knowing what might turn up at Shewalton sandpits on a later summer day, at the start of the autumn migrations. A part of his ideal imagined world now consisted of nothing but springs in which all he did was set up hides at nests all around Annick Lodge, with no danger ever of them being vandalised. A rookery stood above a small marsh where moorhens nested in the valley and he fantasised about building a hide up in the treetops and spending long hours up there with those congenial corvids cawing and tailspreading on every side, swaying high above the earth.

In the previous winter when he'd discovered the Lesser Yellowlegs he'd met an old lady interested in birds who went to Scottish Ornithologist's Club meetings in the winter in Ayr and offered to take him. They had visiting speakers and one of them had been, that winter, a photographer from up the Garnock valley who arranged a full astonishing panoply of Nikon lenses and cameras on the table in front of him before he gave his talk and showed a whole range of amazing images—Barn Owl in flight among the rafters of a house, an Oystercatcher nesting on the hollowed-out top of a fencepost, orange and black and white against the lush, out-of-focus green of an Ayrshire field... The photographer somehow knew all the estate owners in the valley and had got permission to photograph and set up hides and equipment on their land. He would drive around the countryside in a landrover, taking photographs of the birds out of the rolled-down windows, a powerful lens resting on bean bags on the window's edge. For Jed, it was an image of a perfect life.

That night he was driven home with his mind lit and flickering with the bright images. The car headlights made a tunnel of stark brilliance down all the lanes ahead when the old lady took the quieter Ayrshire backroads.

—Those were lovely photographs, she said.

—Yes.

The photographer had been a flamboyant character, flicking up on the screen images of himself baretorsoed before putting on a wetsuit to enter a loch

PLATE 24

CUCKOO

to take photographs of grebes. Even then Jed knew that all these things, in quite that way, would be beyond him. He was not born to them.

The old lady was a social worker. Her husband had a damaged leg and spent long periods in the local Croft Inn, the pub at the end of the village, Springside, where the main Irvine to Kilmarnock road passed. He revelled in the salt bite of the stories among unemployed men who had nothing. He had been wounded in the Second World War.

The old lady dropped Jed off at the bottom of the drive up to the caravan site in the darkness. It was a soft, silent Ayrshire night. A few stars glimmered in and out among shifting clouds. That night he lay in the dark with his mind still alive with photographs from the evening and freshly aware of the misery of his situation and that of his father, sensing for the first time perhaps the older man's unhappiness. One evening the previous summer a small group of foreign tourists, French he thought, young campers, had come to the caravan door just as he was going out.

—You have change? one of them asked.

—I don't, he said. —Just wait a minute. He was eager to help these people holidaying in his country on this softly lit summer evening.

—There's some people at the door here asking if we've got any change, he said at the door to his father. His father came out, took in the young expectant group, and said abruptly:

—No. No change, and closed the door on them.

Jed was left outside with the group of open-faced young people.

—I'm sorry, he said. I'm sorry. He walked away. It was the close-minded, truculent abruptness of it, the unreasonableness, that affected him. It was out of a world in which there was no grace, in which grace and graciousness had been lost, far back, in some lit past where there had still been possibilities for life. He felt embarrassed to be associated with it.

His father would be up at six am, five days a week and also on Sundays. Sometimes the clink of the teaspoon as his father stirred his mug of tea entered the boy's consciousness as he lay drowsing in his bedroom. His father did little else it seemed to him but watch television, even in the spring and summer, closing the curtains in the living room as the planet on its tilted axis, in its massive rotation, dipped the sun to the horizon. His father would sit there in the semi-dark, the light of summer refused. It was an image, though he was not to know it then, that when recalled, many years later, would fill Jed with horror—space and air and actual life refused in favour of the flickering screen and the canned laughter of something produced by others for which his father was the passive recipient, in the light tinged by the orange curtains as the sun shone through them and they glowed.

But sometimes his father would be crouched over some fankle of wires with a glass loupe, black plastic holding a lens plugged over one eye and held in place by his tightened eye socket, wheezily concentrating as he examined the back of a radio or other contraption. The previous winter his father had stripped the filaments from an old electric blanket and, connecting them to a battery, wrapped them round the outside pipes to help stop them freezing.

★

The great lushness of the summer was thickening. The first lime freshness of the Ayrshire beeches and the papery flimsiness of their leaves had toughened and darkened. All over the landscape of Annick the birds were now raising chicks. Consumption, corruption! When the school exams petered out and the pupils all entered the lit space of the summer he felt a terror of unpreparedness in all this fury of breeding and action, the terror of an unfocused life, the terror of being poor and unable. Along with the summer tourists who would camp overnight or for several days on their way to the Highlands, folk from the cities with summer caravans on the site would

PLATE 54

YOUNG OF THE
RASORES & GRALLATORES

arrive for the season. He remembered the son of one family who was reputed to be a championship cyclist en route to cycling across Europe and would pass on his way to the shower block—a compact image of perfect physique with everything ordered and in place, Jed imagined, in his life. Jed aspired and was attracted to such images of perfection as he saw them then. They were like the championship players of Wimbledon in their pure tennis whites.

He was caught up in the summer heat and the moil of the moment. Millions of leaves all round held out their green cages for the light. The barley rose in a green lake in the fields and the summer woods were full of the cries of the small birds which had just left their nests. He was here in this place at this time but felt that all other times were also present, passing in the minds of those alive in them—the big house where one of the two sisters had been stung on the lip by a wasp at a garden party, one summer afternoon, and died; the night of the fire that had razed that house to the ground; the decades ahead here, on an afternoon of rustling leaves, when he would be a memory—they all existed somehow in their own time and place. But *now*, or the procession of moments that made up *now*, were what, in the end, he had.

★

The hot Ayrshire nights of July and August. Up on its hilltop, set back from the road, the little site became a hubbub of campers and summer tourists arriving, unpacking, erecting tents with clinking of tent poles and laughter in their long strip of ground over the thick hedge that bordered the area for caravans in the west. Beyond it, the land sloped down to fields and beyond them were the woods of Annick and beyond them, visible in the Firth and a soft granular gray, were the epic peaks of Arran, lit and gentle in the great hall of air when the sun descended in that direction in the evening and, in the winter, bleak often, in snow that contrasted starkly against their black ridges. When he had first seen those summits he could hardly believe that they existed in Britain. They were like something from Tibet, or out of a picture book. Often the rainmist or the squalls that could stampede in from the west, hammering all the roofs where he was, then moving on and drumming the crossroads at Cunninghamhead, and further, while he stood in a blaze of light, hid Arran's peaks; but they were always there, a grand geological background to the brevity of all the organic life milling around at their base. They were like the near-immortal stars in the W. H. Davies poem, wondering at how close, from a stellar perspective, our cradles were to graves. Yet the sand on the beach could have been mountains once. It was all relative.

None of which occurred to him or the campers in their nightly mêlée and gentle clatterings. Sometimes in the still warmth of the July dusk he would walk along the gravel track of this strip of land where the campers could pitch tent on either side, his feet crunching on the stones still warm from the day's heat, simply for the interest of seeing who had come in that evening, for they were like migratory birds, stopping overnight at some oasis or watering point for rest and refreshment before lighting out for all their undetermined destinations. Murmurs of their voices, occasional laughter, the clink of glasses, from under the canvas; Altair, Deneb and Vega, stars of summer, brightening overhead; the young tawny owls that had now scattered from a nest he had so far not been able to find, calling from the wooded slope across the valley with their husky 'kee-wick!' cries that had a slight squelchiness to them, interspersed with the yowls and quavering notes of the adults. The fierce energy of the planet. Moths whirring palely among the dusk umbellifers. Occasionally a late car would arrive up the drive, hundreds of moths and other insects flickering incandescently across the projected brilliant beam of the headlights. The earthly multitudes. Sometimes on these late wanderings among the human murmurings of unknown lives, passing the sudden perfume of honeysuckle rising like an island of scent in the warm summer night, he would feel compelled to break into a run and then a sprint at the limit of his speed, down the quarter mile of the drive to where it met the Irvine to Stewarton road in the darkness. He would stop there, bending forward with his palms on his knees, right in the centre of the empty main road, delighted by the anarchy of it, sucking the sweet cool air deep into his lungs, then straightening and tilting his head back, his face open to the clear night sky and the Universe, his breathing and heartbeat returning to normal. Then he would walk back up the drive feeling the exhilaration of the young body supercharged with hormones.

He was now seventeen. He would walk, for the pleasure of the summer night, the site lane that wove around the caravans, and slip into the dark caravan where his parents slept at one end and his sisters at the other, he in the bedroom adjacent to them. There, among bird skulls, feathers and the dissections of pellets under the bed, to the slow background fading of the campers' voices somewhere far, he would fall asleep. The following morning early, all that erecting and clinking of tent poles of the campers would be reversed, as the sun rose into the haze with its savage and unforgiving blaze. The sun was not interested in failure. People were dying and enduring heartbreak and receiving terrifying prognoses, opening letters delivered by cheerful postmen freighted with the terrible every morning; that local star made no allowances for any of it with its implacable light and heat, which turned the little ponds all across the landscape, like that at Sevenacres Mill or below the quarry above Dundonald where the leaves were grey with whinstone dust, to a hot broth seething with larvae; and drew, as if with a magical gesture, the dragonfly nymphs up out of the mud to cling motionless to the early morning stems, there to wrap their six legs round rushes and undergo the small violence of transformation, the pale crumpled wings on their backs like buds growing and stiffening as Jed grew and stiffened nightly before sleep and again when he

woke in the morning. The sun did not modify itself
to what anyone thought or felt. He understood this
pristine barbarity instinctually though he could not
have described it then. You had to run to keep up
with the sun. You had to guard against trouble.
The art of life is the art of avoiding pain. Where had he
read that? In one of the books in the library at the
town hall he escaped girls from. *What do you use for
contraception—personality?* went the old insult.

In his case it was true, his personality being shy-
ness and sheer ignorance. While many of his male
contemporaries were shuddering and spurting between the thighs of their girlfriends, the wet thick
milk splashed onto the growing hairs of his belly
and lower chest, filling his navel with liquid pearl.
Sometimes he smelt it on his fingertips: it smelt of
freshness and newness, this liquid, opaque and clari-
fying, seething with the infinitesimal spermatozoa
as the hot broth of the ponds whirled with larvae.
It was the energy of the sun too and would not be
outwitted. It was part of the human comedy that
this force should be fiercest and fullest when humans were least able to understand it intellectually
or psychologically. In an earlier age or in a different
incarnation he could have been a father at eighteen
with six or seven children by the time he was an old
man at thirty. But Catholicism saved him with its
iron press. Who knows how many achievements or
accomplishments, even if they all come to nothing
finally in the light of the indifferent sun, are only
made possible by awkwardness or repression, shy-
ness or ineptitude? The sun, that blazing star that

lifted out of the haze on the July morning, cared
nothing for any of that. It was merely a match that
put its flame to a great city made of dry tinder. It
cared nothing for consequences.

★

Among all this was the caravan site's Circe or Aph-
rodite. She was married and lived at the end of the
row of caravans they lived on. She was the lushness
of the planet and at one with the hot seething buzz-
ing life of the hedges now in July, and she threatened in imagination if not in real life to pull him
down into that bare seething heat where he would
be lost and dissolved. She was aware, he sensed,
of her effect. Sometimes she would sunbathe at
the front of her caravan and he would pass by and
not be able to look, apart from a mere glance. He
was frightened of what would happen to him if he
looked. It would be like looking at the sun full on
through binoculars. Her presence there was a constant source of interest and animation, quite as en-
livening as the tawny owls in the witchwood over
the river. She would drive around in the summer,
though she was married, with another neighbour,
an electronics expert who fixed medical machines
in hospitals and worked unusual hours, till one day
he stopped. He took to fixing cars in front of his
caravan, propping their wheel-less frames up on
bricks and began to gather an improbable collection
of stray cats. Jed had asked him if he would be able
to build him a high-speed flash unit for photogra-

phy and he said he could, though in the absence of money this never happened. The man did, though, give him an entire collection of *Time-Life* photography volumes for nothing. Photography had at one time been important to the man but meant little to him now. Jed would pore, meditatively, with the energy of his live interest, through these examples of a world made reasonable and beautiful.

The woman moved away with her husband, and the man became gradually shabbier and more oil-stained and unwashed. An ever-increasing disorder overcame him. The boy had read about entropy, the tendency of things to move towards disorder and dissolution. Everything had to be tidied and put back into its place constantly. The world was a continual battle against this drift towards chaos. The man had given up on this battle. He was later found dead, sitting upright on his couch, in a shambles of a caravan, in subzero temperatures wearing three pairs of trousers and surrounded by the purring and solicitous entourage, their tails upright, rubbing themselves against the discoverer's legs, of twenty cats.

Jed could barely endure the pattern of the long summer days without routine and habit and a project. He had to feel, by having done some activity, however meaningless it was really in the light of geological time, that he deserved to eat. He had to feel an honest tiredness. He was like a cat that needed to flex its claws against the trunk of a tree, sinking the curved needles into the irregular bark with a satisfying extremity. It was turning to August; the great planetary migrations were beginning. He took to cycling to Shewalton Sandpits every afternoon. The first autumn migrants were moving through. Greenshanks sometimes rose from the margins of the pits with their startle-white rumps and their call—'chu-chu-chu'—the three quick flute notes— and would glide to their alighting onto the margin of the pits' other side, to stand alert, immediately bobbing. Then each would calm and begin pacing along the shadows, picking at this or that invisible item before it. Each had the whole sky but the blue open lens of the pit pulled them down as surely as photons stream down to an eye.

He liked the unexpectedness of these afternoon visits in the August heat and light, banks of rosebay willowherb igniting up their tall towers leaving in their wake the fluffy pods of the seeds that the breezes teased out and blew away as they did the heads of the thistles. The endless fecundity. You never knew what would turn up. Five greenshank one day; another, a spotted redshank, or two bar-tailed godwits, larger and gracefuller. Green Tiger beetles emerged from the sandy soil of this pit in May in the first flare of heat, light metallic green insects with golden secateur jaws, advancing suddenly in little jerky sprints across the ground, or taking to the air with a sudden heat-stirred buzz. And the camouflaged spiders that lived in burrows in the sand stalked across their little plains under the sympetrum dragonflies that poised, red or yellow-thoraxed, swivelling the big head, all eye, around its fixed axis and angling the four wings, light and rustly as discarded cellophane from cigarette packets, forward. Then they would

BLACK TAILED GODWIT.

Summer

Winter

leap, noiselessly, into the air at some passing fly, often returning to the same small twig-perch. They were like miniature machines, whirring and entirely beyond emotion.

A constant at the back of his head was a tussle for lightness and order. He was also waiting for something to happen, though he did not know what. He would wonder sometimes later how many people went on in expectation of some event or encounter that would change everything or angle them down a path they would not otherwise have gone. He would lie in the dark puzzling about these things: how had he come to be him? Why was he himself and not his father, or the neighbour's dog, or one of the owls in the witchwood sending out its long quavering call under Orion and Sirius? It was just how it was. When he traced it all back, everything that had ever happened anywhere had led to his lying in the little bed with his overactive brain. Some event eighty years ago that he could know nothing of, some afternoon in Belfast or in Glasgow, when his paternal grandfather had taken one turn rather than another, or slept in, or not slept in and, however it happened, had met the woman he would marry. Some similar turn of events in the minutiae of being alive and the billions of daily interactions had also happened on his mother's side with her own parents. The same thing had happened between Jed's own parents. Take that back right to the start of humans, for everyone, and not just him, these uncountable coincidences, and you had the world they were in. Sometimes he would be filled with terror at the thought of all this, and how one move in one direction, some seemingly inconsequential thing, could lead on to something that could affect him for life. It was the weight of action, the weight of the world.

A few years earlier when he was thirteen the other boy on the caravan site when he still talked to him—they had had a falling out since—had shown him in his boy's way a ten-pence piece flat and thin as a sheet of paper.

—How did that happen?

—You put it on the railway line. The train goes over it.

—Isn't that dangerous?

—Na. I can show you.

They had been out along the railway line near what had been the old railway station at Cunninghamhead—buildings and platforms where the trains once stopped and people stepped out, in an almost Edwardian grace and civility before the cataclysm of the First World War, on May afternoons of wild-flowered hedges and built white clouds. Now it was nothing but dried grasses and occasionally strawberries you could find among it all where the garden of the stationmaster's house had been.

There was a train coming along the line from the direction of Kilmarnock, full of passengers you could glimpse in window after window as the carriages roared and clattered by. You could hear the faint, telltale buzz or vibration on the line of something momentous and huge that was approaching and would soon be here.

—Watch, the other boy said. He took a small metal drum that had held cooking oil, dumped in the wasteground of the old station, and leaned it against the rail.

—Are you sure about that? Jed said.

—Calm doon. It's fine. Ahve done this loads a times.

—Loads.

—Aye. Watch whit happens.

They hid behind the embankment. For a few moments he considered running out onto the track and taking the drum off the line. But the moment for that impulse passed and was subdued and overborne by the awareness of the train powering ever closer to this point of impact. He was uneasy but not to have gone along with it would have meant loss of face. He would have been branded a feartie.

The train approached—they could tell by the increasing hum and vibration in the tracks. It hit the drum full on. There was a scatter of sparks and the drum was thrown to one side. The train continued on its way and was soon off into the unblaming distance.

—See? Telt ye.

In the silence that followed they crept out onto the irregular whinstone gravel the tracks and sleepers were bedded on, and examined the drum. It had a big dent in it.

—Luk at that. Ya beauty.

Suddenly as they stood there, there was a man in a mid-blue tracksuit entering the old station wasteground and running towards them. It was authority from the other world, a voice to pluck them back into a harsher universe.

It was too late for them to run.

—Did you boys do that? the man said in a raised voice. —Did you boys put that drum on the line? He had short grey hair, sharp features and an official manner.

—Naw, the other boy said instantly. —We just heard the soond o it.

The man seemed unconvinced. He said, with weight:

—Because whoever did could have caused a major accident and derailed that train. People could have been killed. Whoever did it—and here he paused for emphasis—could have ended up in prison.

It was clear that they were deeply under suspicion but that the man had no evidence apart from their proximity to the passing train.

—Aye, said the other boy. Whoever did that musta been crazy. It wisny us.

The man turned away, this figure from the adult world, and ran purposefully to where the old station opened onto the main Irvine to Stewarton road. Soon he was a dot of blue under the tall sky with its soft white clouds, running towards Stewarton.

—That guy didny ken onyhin, the other boy said. But Jed knew that they had been lucky and that his not wanting to be considered a feartie in other circumstances could have changed the course of his life in a dreadful direction. As it was, they went on into the evening, free of any involvement or interference from the full weight of the world and its laws. He was aware of his stepping carefully over the grasses on the way back up to the caravan site. You had to watch where you put your feet in this world. It was as if they had dared something and gotten away with it and the world after looked a new thing for that revision.

There was a streak of something else in the other boy that Jed generally did not have and soon made him keep his distance. He had once been with him on the aqueduct above the river. They looked over and there far below was a group of other teenagers. Without warning, the boy scooped up a handful of the big whinstane pebbles and tossed them over the bridge. There was a shriek from below and the boy Jed was with immediately sprinted away along the track towards the little bridge of the site lane where it crossed above the railway line. Jed had no choice but to do the same, despite his innocence, bound as he was by the other's action. After several hundred yards they stopped, panting, bending over with their hands on their knees.

—What the fuck did you...do...that for?

The other boy was laughing through his wheezing breaths.

—It's awright. Naebuddy can catch us.

—You could have put someone's eye out back there! Maybe you even did!

—That wouldny have happened. It's fine.

—It's not fine. I could have got the blame for it as well, and I didn't do anythin. I wasn't interested in doin anythin.

The other boy seemed entirely unmoved at the idea that by tossing the stones over the bridge someone could have been seriously injured. It was an indication to Jed of the different levels in what people considered acceptable, that one person could cut off somone's limb with as little compunction as killing a fly, while another stepped around the big hairy caterpillars crossing the drive up to the caravan site from grass jungle to grass jungle to avoid giving hurt.

On another occasion they had been out on their bikes cycling into a wind, when they passed a boy on the verge. Jed's companion was in front and, as he passed, he coolly turned his head and spat in the walking boy's face, then accelerated on, pedalling with renewed energy.

Jed was following sharp behind, too startled to stop, with no choice as he saw it but also to accelerate past the boy, an unwitting accomplice in what looked like a planned maneouvre. A half a mile on, after a long freewheeling slope that the first boy took with his hands and arms raised in the air, as they stood astride the crossbars of their bikes, Jed said:

—That's it. That's the last time I'm coming out with you.

—What's the problem? the other said. —He hud it comin.

—Had what comin? Bein spat at in the face? That's disgustin! You didn't even know him!

He wondered where it came from, this streak of—what was it? Evil? Male energy gone wrong?

There had been a day when he was fourteen coming up the drive to the site after school, early spring, ahead of his sisters and stepbrother straggling behind. A big grey silent afternoon. He strode along the caravan path and leapt up onto the steps. The door was open and his mother came out to meet him in her humming happiness.

—Mum, mum, he said as a joke, D———'s missing. He wasn't on the bus!

His mother's expression clanged shut as if a portcullis had dropped. —What? Where is he?

—I'm only kidding. It was just a joke, mum.

—That's no joke Ger'd. You could have given me a heart attack.

—I'm sorry mum. I just got it in my head to say it. I thought it would be funny.

—It was not funny. Don't you go doin that again.

But where had the impulse come from? Something about his mother's calm and humming contentment—she always hummed and sang snatches of hymns to herself when she was happy—had prompted him, entirely unpremeditatedly.

★

But he had been waiting for something to happen that August of willowherb and rustling heat and white clouds.

One afternoon he was down at Irvine harbour. The birds were starting to come back to the estuary at Bogside flats across the water. There were two small figures out walking under the huge sky with what seemed to be binoculars. It was a mark of his own isolation that he immediately cycled the two miles around, left his bike among the whins, crossed the railway track and walked the high river bank to where it descended and opened out to the mudflats of the estuary. He met the two young men coming

in the opposite direction, obviously the birdwatchers, from the binoculars around their necks.

He had met one of them before, a man who had
come along to Irvine Royal's Ornithologist's Club
meetings in the Biology hut after school. Another
man had also appeared on one of these meetings,
the son of a florist from Kilwinning who produced
things from his pockets like a sparrowhawk's foot and
lower leg and spoke in a strange mix of half-code to
the other man, referencing different characters in the
area who were involved with birds. It was a glimpse
into another world for the boy. The man was as pe-
remptory and definite in his opinions and speeches as
a hawk—deeply appealing to an uncertain young-
ster, though he had been treated with what seemed a
respectful scepticism by the other man.

Now here he was, that other man, with his brother, on a day when the waders were starting to re-
gather on the estuary.

—Anything interesting? Jed asked.

—Just the usual, the man's brother said. Peewits.
Redshanks. Dunlin. Couple of bar-tailed godwits.

Over the Bogside flats and the racecourse, flocks
of lapwings rose with their flickering black and
white wings.

—You should come to the house and see us, said
the first brother. We're just beside the school.

So one afternoon in the following week, he rang
their doorbell. The younger brother answered and
he was taken up two flights of stairs to the top room
they shared, with a window looking from a vantage
down onto the street. Great things would be discussed

PLATE II.

WAXWING OR BOHEMIAN CHATTERER.

from their loft room—expeditions to the Falklands, to Antarctica. They both took photographs and from them Jed picked up by natural conversation some of what he learned about photography. The upper room was spacious and calm, away from the rest of the house—a small example of the grace and civility he did not have in his caravan bedroom, but they offered it to him freely. They would all scrutinise the partwork *Birds of the World*, filed in black ringbinders, on bleak winter afternoons of unwalkable weather and coolly and ruthlessly assessed the quality of its bird photographs from their privileged viewpoint of uninvolved critics. This bedroom and its brothers opened another room in the boy's head, a further dimension, and it offered a bolthole at points from the reality of his caravan life up country. Each Sunday morning he would set out and walk the four miles into the town and often be gone till late evening, walking the four miles home again, often with a ten-mile walk along Irvine shore in the middle of the day. One morning he had found a dead short-eared owl at the roadside, newly hit by a car, but the big buff and barred softness of it was entirely unmarked.Its fierce orange eyes with their black pupils surrounded by the vivid facial disk markings were still open. It looked as if, wide-eyed, it was still alive. He had sat it along his right forearm and held it down by the tail with his other hand, and walked on into the quiet Sunday morning town, occasionally passed by drivers unsure of what they'd seen, a boy with an amber-eyed owl on his arm.

He reached the brothers' house. The front door

was open, and when he rang the doorbell there was always a pause and then the blurry figure of one of the brothers appeared at the far end of the lobby and rapidly enlarged beyond the frosted glass of the inner door as he approached to open it from within. He swung the door open with the big, expectant half-smile typical of this action.

His expression, falling on the owl, changed as if he'd been struck by silent lightning.

—Jesus Christ. It's no alive—is it?

—No. It just looks it.

They had spent the afternoon in the top room photographing the bird: the huge ear cavities, the size of a cat's, hidden behind the flap of the facial disc and set at a different height on each side of the head.

★

That winter, out of old bits of wood cast up on the shoreline of the estuary, they built a hide at the edge of Bogside Flats. As the tide slowly intrickled, running over the sand in a froth-edged lace, carrying small white recurved gull breast feathers on its moving surface, the small waders, redshanks and dunlin, would follow its progress, crisscrossing at the edge, picking at this or that marine worm with a dart, or sinking their beaks into the sand like a sword into a scabbard. They came right up to the bottom of the hide, five feet away. The three young men looked down through the slat they'd left in the wood. He was amazed as he always would be at the pristine perfection of these birds, at their state of apparent

GREY PHALAROPE

Winter

Summer

Stewart Del.

Lizars Sc.

perfect health, at the superb detail and marking of their feathers. In the autumn a group of Little Stints had passed through. You could tell them by their diminutive size and the pale streaks up and over their backs—tiny wading birds so intent on feeding that the three young men stood in the shallows watching them feed frantically from three or four feet away. It was a slant-lit September afternoon, still warm in the sunlight, and of an almost holy stillness. The incoming tide was like a mirror and at the edge of the advancing water, pacing backwards and forwards, aware of but ignoring the three of them, so intent were they on fattening for the long migrations, the miniature wading birds moved. A high passenger jet went over in the blue, somehow accentuating the wide, estuarine silence. It was happiness, that hour with the three of them softly exclaiming at their good luck at the enforced tameness of the little wading birds. Then the tide reached the edge of the saltmarsh, and the stints, five or six of them, flew off.

—What was that like?! Just tremendous! The wee beauties!

—Yes, he said. In the presence of his effusive friends he was able to vocalise his enthusiasm for these things. It woke up something inside him. It was like a fire slowly being kindled that had lain, set unlit in a grate, for a long time.

And here were the birds on their way to whatever exotic places for the winter, stopping over at Irvine. The two brothers had a poor view of the banality of the town which Jed had also intuited but never put into words. But the estuary and the harbour were

THE DUSKY TOTANUS.

Summer.

Winter.

PLATE 14.

a thing apart from the couthy, sectarian and history-sunk elements of the burgh. These diminutive wading birds that would put hundreds and perhaps thousands of miles under their wings after using the estuary as a stopping point were part of a bigger thing, something that cared not a whit for human history, pain or grief.

That winter he had taken part in the Birds of Estuaries Enquiry for the British Trust for Ornithology: weekly counts one Saturday morning a month of the numbers of different species of waders at Bogside Flats. With almost godlike optimism, hundreds of amateur ornithologists put faith in their ability to count hundreds and often thousands of wading birds accurately as they turned and twisted in flight in their frantic groups or flickered in high dark masses against the grey sky in the distance. He made weekly bar charts, colouring them in with a different colour for each species—redshank, dunlin, curloo, lapwing, sanderling, oystercatcher, bar-tailed godwit, shelduck—taking a mild satisfaction in the description of the shifting thousands by numbers.

Bogside was an exciting place, a gathering ground for autumn and over-wintering waders congregated again from their far-flung nesting grounds. The winter huddlers in pubs all over the town were like them, except the birds recognised no time or date. They lived by the incoming and outgoing tides. The scrawny, sinewy wild spirits in the wide spaces of Atlantic air answered something in him. It was as if he felt he was one of them or he could be one of them and so could never be lost, not really. They were the real world.

THE COMMON SHEILDRAKE

The two brothers had a Fensman hide. One winter day they put it up on one of the little saltmarsh islands that the birds crowded onto at high tide, driven there by the surrounding water which gradually rose and left them a smaller and smaller area of dry saltmarsh to rest on. Jed and one of the brothers left the other inside and retreated to the wooden hide they'd built out of old driftwood, a draughty and chill structure occasionally creaking bleakly when the wind moved through its slits. Through binoculars they could see the birds slowly congregating around the hide where the second brother sat, gazing through a lens, and they wondered what he was experiencing, that separate hidden consciousness peering through the viewfinder of a camera. What was it all about, that desire? Was it a form of voyeurism, a need to glimpse into that secret world of jostling and sleeping beaks tucked in their backs, to be among them and carry some trophy back as a record of the adventure, having dared the chaos and made it back again safe to the comprehensible human world with its timetables and attempted-decent laws? Afterwards, the gales could rage and the torrents fall, but you would have escaped back into your own dimension with the prize, whether images or a memory, and barely cared.

There was something salving to him in those birds on the winter estuary, an everyday revelling bleakness that was like a swabbing calm smirr to the spikes of heat and energy that were already leaping in him. He was not to know it then but at intervals throughout his life this sense would recur. Many years in his future there would be a morning on an Atlantic island, a grey morning of overall mizzling wet and the roaring of the sea, when he had a soothing sense of what it would be like to go off in that and be lost in it forever. It did not ask anything of him; in its undemandingness it removed some of the responsibility of being, whereas a day on that same island of astonishing loveliness, of heat and cobalt ocean and tall white clouds, somehow demanded of him an equal action in which he must always fall short.

★

February. He had stepped off the bus at the lane end and was walking up the drive to the caravan site, with the big broken-strapped satchel stuffed with books tucked under his right arm. The snowdrops were dying. Deep in the earth other seeds were stirring, undetected. The glossy green leaves shaped like arrowheads or stylised hearts of the Lords and Ladies colonies were sprouting in the bare beechwoods across the Annick Water and under hedges and in the mixed wood past Annick Lodge. In May, the green rolled-up spears of the flowers would unroll, quickly, to the cowled spathes and the purple spadix in the centre, smelling of dung and hot to the touch, ready for *Psychoda phalaenoides*, a tiny fly, to pollinate them. Then they would wither to the red waxy berries, bright as a clown's lips.

But this was February. There would be a frost. The first stars were sparking out in the tall blue of the Universe. It would sometimes come to him, the realisation that this was his life, what he had to work with, but always it was separated from him by an invisible screen, or it was like trying to pick up the little spilled globules of mercury in the chemistry class, half-liquid and half-metal, whose bright silver evaded your fingertips on the incised wooden desk with its gas taps. The sun had left an afterglow in the west, a huge radiance that was like a silent expression of astonishment at something enormous and withdrawn into the distance. A song thrush was up in a silhouetted bough, against that pale blue, streaked above with pink, somewhere in the minute intricacies of black twigs. Its notes rang out in the land's silence. *Spring is coming! Spring is coming! Can you hear it? Can you hear it? So I am singing because I know! So I am singing because! Yes I am! Yes I am!*

He stood and listened for a few minutes, then he walked down the path to the caravan with the big light of the west on his face, and entered the troubled space.

A manuscript page from the first draft.
The text here appears at the foot of page 23 *et seq.*

An Afterword

THE FIRST DRAFT OF this book was handwritten in an A4 hardback Moleskine notebook in six weeks in the spring and summer of 2018 and, for pen geeks, with a 1938 Pelikan 100N with an extra-fine nib, unfortunately trashed a few years ago when I dropped it, point-first, onto a kitchen floor. I wrote this text for two main reasons: to explain something of my background to a young person— obviously for when she was much older—whom I got to know quite well for a few years; and to make peace of sorts, insofar as that's ever possible, with this book's central character—confused, baffled and ignorant as he is. The book is, generally speaking, memoir, and most of it is 'true'; yet even in memoir, imagination, invention, and sheer misremembering have their place. So to have written Jed as 'myself', in the first person, would have felt inaccurate. The third person narrative was a useful way of differentiating him from me as author; not only in time, but in character. With the proviso accepted that this book should not be considered wholly documentary, the attitudes in it are nonetheless true to the ethos of its period: the early-to-mid 1970s.

One thing which has seen a massive shift against a background of environmental near-collapse is attitudes toward the natural world, here shown by the brief account of egg-collecting and the symbolism of the bird's egg. There is an interesting, if depressing, sociological history, some of it class-related, behind this now universally condemned activity as it was practised in the late 1800s and the first half of the twentieth century. Jed in *The Ayrshire Nestling* was a schoolboy egg-collector for a few years, moving on, when a strengthening moral sense made him ashamed, to other natural history interests. In this he formed part of a long tradition which includes now-famous naturalists; öological dilettantes for whom this collecting instinct was a route into wider, more socially acceptable interest in natural history and conservation. There is a big difference between the brief enthusiasms of a schoolboy and the obsession of the true öologist, which, in those possessed by it, frequently lasted a lifetime. Reading about these individuals can be disturbing; in the late nineteenth century and the first half of the twentieth, such men—and they were almost exclusively men, an interesting psychological fact in itself—would, unlike the schoolboy, find no value in taking a single egg from a nest; instead they would pillage whole clutches, and not only whole clutches, but *series* of clutches of a single species, often proudly exhibiting them at meetings of öological societies. A contemporary reader of such accounts is likely to be horrified by the rapacity of such scenarios, which many of the collectors of the time tried to justify to themselves as extending scientific knowledge. Like expert computer hackers later using their skills on the side of law and order, many of these collectors became extraordinarily adept field naturalists, as well as hardy, tough, and capable of surviving spartan conditions in remote landscapes. The noted ornithologist Desmond Nethersole-Thompson, for instance, began as one such egg-collector. He later used those skills that he had earned money by, selling eggs taken from nests, to find numerous clutches of the notoriously secretive greenshank in the extensive Flow country of Sutherland in some of the wildest landscapes in Britain. His New Naturalist volume *The Greenshank* and other monographs like his books *The Snow Bunting* and *The Dotterel* are considered classics. None of them could have been written without his previous öological experience. Such fieldcraft as he possessed wasn't easily attained; only the lust for eggs—or, as has been pointed out, for egg*shells*— could, arguably, develop it.

It is difficult now to see these activities, in a larger psychological context, as anything other than

a crime against femaleness, of which the egg is a
potent symbol; it may be this which is behind Jed's
guilty destruction of his own small collection in the
context of his mother's action. Two 1940s novels,
The Awl Birds (another name for Avocets; the novel
was also published as *Bledgrave Hall*) and *Adventure Lit
Their Star*, as noted in a fascinating paper by Joanna
C Dobson*, posited the egg-collector as a kind of
subhuman sinner against life, via loosely fictional
accounts: ornithologists guarding nests of then
extremely rare avocets and little ringed plovers from
egg thieves; this in the context of psychological
vulnerabilities regarding land and birds as emblems
of Britishness in a country still reeling from the
Second World War. Museums across the UK now
contain thousands of birds' eggs from donated
historical collections; they are seldom displayed,
attended as they are by a sort of shame, guilt and
perhaps unease that their beauty could encourage
unwelcome interest.

A word about the illustrations in this book. These
are all from one source, the Scottish naturalist Sir
William Jardine's groundbreaking (at the time) series
The Naturalist's Library, published in forty volumes
by William Lizars of Edinburgh, between 1833 and
1843. The illustrations in the *Nestling* are from four
of these related to British birds. Around 2011 in a
bric-a-brac shop in Stroud, Gloucestershire, I found

---

*Dobson, Joanna C.: '"A Menace to England": The Egg Collec-
tor as Arch-Villain in Two 1940s Bird Novels'; *Literature & History*,
2021, Vol. 3(2), pp121–137.

a group of small, 4 x 6 inch colour plates—of dipper, sparrowhawk, curlew and snow bunting—salvaged from water-damaged volumes and being sold for £5 each. Struck by their quality, I bought them, later using the images in my capacity as a designer and typographer for private homemade correspondence cards. In spring 2023, browsing the web, I happened on a few reasonably priced volumes from *The Naturalist's Library* for sale. The images are public domain, though not widely available unless one can access the books themselves. One volume that came into my hands is signed in flourished copperplate by its owner, the resonantly named Horatio Vertue, and inscribed 'May 1839'; a little online sleuthing reveals that Mr Vertue, who would have been 24 at the time he signed this volume, later went to South Africa, dying there at the age of 90 in October 1905; the book now bears the bookplate of one Francis Hemmings, a taxonomic specialist who latterly named a genus of butterflies in honour of Vladimir Nabokov—another assiduous collector in a now-shamed activity. Each volume has some thirty bird engravings, of remarkable fidelity to their subjects for the time and extremely finely detailed. They are 'hand-coloured'; hand-colouring, as far as I can ascertain, was often carried out by women and children, who must have had considerable skill; effectively they turned each copy of an individual plate, which *could* be mass-produced, into its own artwork, albeit with only minor differences between the same plates in different copies; a different world from the mass productions of contemporary colour printing. Comparing the dipper and snow bunting plates bought in Stroud as salvaged offcuts with the same engravings in the published volume, as I was able to, is to see subtle differences: a stripe of blue in one, absent from the other; scapulars painted brown in one, left in the other as plain paper, untouched. The work involved in such hand-colouring must have been major: some of the Jardine volumes were reputed to have sold several thousand copies. One thinks of those nameless hand-colourists, uncredited in the volumes, and wonders. I confess that some plates' presences in this book are as much decorative as directly illustrative of Jed's developing interest in birds; I felt they were too beautiful not to include.

The caravan site in this account was real. Back in the seventies Cunninghamhead Estate, on the Irvine to Stewarton road, was a somewhat ramshackle place, albeit set within the grounds of a former walled garden and surrounded by woods and fields; the foundations of its big house, which burned down in a fire, could still be seen. The former caravan park in all its eccentric gaiety and oddness has now gone 'upmarket' and is basically a retirement home; the caravans have become static mobile homes resembling small bungalows. I have occasionally revisited and walked around with friends, dubiously regaling them with scenes from my past. 'Look!' I will say—for I bought cheaply my own caravan there in 1977 after leaving my family's, described in this account—'that's the telegraph pole that had to be installed beside my caravan in 1983, so a phone line could be put in and I could make phone calls as a freelance writer working for *Reader's Digest*.' The landscape round about, on the other hand, is relatively unchanged, though Middleton Farm, where Jed singled neeps, and Fairliecrevoch, are both now small complexes of private dwellings, no longer working farms. And the floodpool where the lesser yellowlegs turned up is now unrecognisable: it is a small forest of alder trees.

The gloomy sublimity of Edward Thomas's lines:

> When I look back I am like moon, sparrow, and mouse
> That witnessed what they could never understand
> Or alter or prevent in the dark house

has always resonated with me. They can serve as an epigraph to Jed and these few years of his story. There he is, spotlit in a way he would have detested, and like the famous sparrow in Bede's account, flitting briefly between two darknesses through the lighted hall.

Acknowledgements

I thank the earlier readers of this account, Sheila Wakefield of Red Squirrel Press, James McGonigal (also my first reader when I was fifteen years old), and Pip Osmond-Williams, for friendship, valuable overviews and feedback; that force, performance poet and writer Jenny Lindsay, who read enthusiastically the obsessive and neurotic account of this young Ayrshire lad, for judging that 'even the jizzy bits werenae misogyny'; the scholar and poet Petra Johana Poncarová for her friendship and for insightful comments on the t/s at a later stage; and especially Geraldine Clarkson, who brought to a close reading of the text in its closing stages her characteristic attention to detail, appreciation and enthusiasm—all qualities evident in her own often-remarkable poetry and other writings.

Thanks are due, too, to poet, editor and lecturer Naush Sabah for her friendship and general encouragement, and to my old Ayrshire pal and poet Cheryl Follon; both have had the 'Cambridge tour' of the caravan site as it is now and have borne my witterings on about it with good grace and uncharacteristic stoicism.

My deep thanks too to Steve Cook and David Swinburne, Co-Directors of Education at the mighty Royal Literary Fund based in London; their unobtrusive support of my work over many years has been an unexpected blessing.

Lastly, and certainly not least, to my exemplary publisher Sheila Wakefield who let me typeset and design my own book, as is my preference, and for her support and enthusiasm throughout for this text, my gratitude.

Biographical Note

Gerry Cambridge's six books of poetry include *Notes for Lighting a Fire* (2012) and *The Light Acknowledgers & Other Poems* (2019), both from HappenStance Press. He founded *The Dark Horse*, Scotland's leading poetry journal, in 1995. He is also an essayist, print designer, typographer, and former nature photographer. He continued to live in a caravan in Ayrshire, adjacent to the one mentioned in this account, from 1977–1997, then left to become Brownsbank Fellow in MacDiarmid's former home for 1997–1999. As a critic he contributed ten essays to the four-volume *Oxford Encyclopaedia of American Literature* (2004) and wrote nine 12,000-word monograph essays for the Gale/Charles Scribner's Sons textbook series *British Writers* and *American Writers* between 2000 and 2006. In his mid-twenties he was, as far as he knows, one of the youngest-ever regular freelancers—specialising in nature articles—for the UK edition of *The Reader's Digest* magazine, which at the time (the 1980s) had a monthly circulation of 1.5 million copies. An Honorary Fellow of the Association for Scottish Literature, he received a Cholmondeley Award for his poetry, administered by the Society of Authors in London, in June 2024. *The Ayrshire Nestling* is his first book of prose.

A NOTE ON THE TYPE

This text is set in Bembo Book, one of the contemporary digital versions of Francesco Griffo's c.1495 typeface cut and used for the Venetian printer Aldus Manutius's edition of the Latin work *De Aetna*, by the Italian scholar and poet Pietro Bembo. It was later accompanied in the 1520s by the italic, a mix of Blado (the italic face for Poliphilus) and a type designed by the calligrapher Giovanni Antonio Tagliente. A version was designed by the typographer Stanley Morison for Monotype and released in 1929, but the digital cut of this can appear a little 'thin' for contemporary printing; Bembo Book, with its extra robustness, was designed to imitate the 'ink squash' of the older metal typeface and print methods. Bembo is a classic, time-honoured typeface, beautifully legible and 'transparent', which does not draw undue attention to itself for a reader.